Jörg Adam, Dominik Harborth
& Andrea Vilter

Second Aid

Doorstops, drip-catchers and other symbiotic gadgets

avedition

Crate handle

Bibliographic information published by *Die Deutsche Bibliothek*

Die Deutsche Bibliothek lists this publication in the *Deutsche Nationalbibliografie*.
For detailed bibliographic data see www.ddb.de

Concept and editing
Jörg Adam, Dominik Harborth & Andrea Vilter

Design of book/exhibition
Adam und Harborth, Berlin

Studio photography
Bernd Gallandi, Berlin

Copy editing
Ivan Vladislavić (English)
Andrea Vilter (German)

Translation
Vineeta Manglani, Lucy James, Ivan Vladislavić, Andrea Vilter

Complete production
Grafisches Zentrum Drucktechnik, Ditzingen and Gotha

The original German edition *Helfershelfer – Türbremse, Tropfenfänger und
andere obligate Symbionten* was published by Edition Solitude, Stuttgart and
Grafisches Zentrum Drucktechnik, Ditzingen in 2000

This publication accompanies the exhibition
'Helfershelfer – Türbremse, Tropfenfänger und andere obligate Symbionten'
by Jörg Adam and Dominik Harborth

ISBN 3-929638-59-2 (www.avedition.com)
Printed in Germany

Once upon a time there were gods only, and no mortal creatures ... But when they [the gods] were about to bring them into the light of day, they ordered Prometheus and Epimetheus to equip them, and to distribute to them severally their proper qualities. Epimetheus said to Prometheus: 'Let me distribute, and do you inspect.' ...

Thus did Epimetheus, who, not being very wise, forgot that he had distributed among the brute animals all the qualities which he had to give – and when he came to man, who was still unprovided, he was terribly perplexed ...

Prometheus, not knowing how he could devise his salvation, stole the mechanical arts of Hephaestus and Athene, and fire with them (they could neither have been acquired nor used without fire), and gave them to man. Thus man had the wisdom necessary to the support of life ... But Prometheus is said to have been afterwards prosecuted for theft ...

from *The Dialogues of Plato*

Introduction

The faculty of handcrafting, which Prometheus stole for us, put us in a position to create individual aids to serve our individual needs. Today, our environment is characterized by such aids, which we give names like 'roll-neck pullover', 'wristwatch', 'chair' or 'aeroplane'. These, too, serve our needs, but they are mostly industrially manufactured mass products, less unique than the people for whom they were developed.

Naturally, the goal of any product development is to take into account all consumer demands if possible. But the demands of various buyers of a product often contradict one another or are mutually exclusive. Already during the development and marketing of a mass product, consideration of the interests of a small group must therefore be subordinated to those of a larger one. However, the relevant group of consumers, let's say 90 per cent of all women and men, is not clearly distinguished from a closed group of 10 per cent, for whom it would be worthwhile to develop an independent product. Rather, a range of different needs are presented, which cannot be addressed by a single product.

The user who has acquired a product he finds inadequate will react in one of three ways, reflecting disappointment with the product as a whole, willingness to accommodate its failings of necessity, or the decision to use another object that fills in the gap: I'm not going to use that dripping coffee pot any more, the user will say; or, I'll wipe the dangling droplet off the spout with my forefinger after every pouring; or, I'll attach a little paper rosette, perhaps also a little sponge, to the spout, to avoid coffee stains on the tablecloth.

The creation of a complementary object, meant to compensate for the 'gap' experienced as a shortcoming or to fulfil a broader user demand, is the moment in which a 'second aid' is born. It is the active, creative intervention of the user in the seemingly hermetic design process: the mass-produced aid acquires an aid – the first aid receives second aid.

The initial form of 'objectifying the gap' may be just an amateurish tinkering, which makes the product suitable for the required use. But the adaptation of an item by means of a second aid will rarely produce something unique. In all areas of life we are offered accessories, customizing kits, updates, attachments, extras and adapters by countless 'independent suppliers'. Inventors, who interpret the fulfilment of their personal demands as a blessing for a (profitable) clientele; mail-order suppliers, who reach millions with their catalogues; or supermarkets displaying ultra-cheap items in the bargain basement or on shelves next to the till – all of these turn second aids into mass products.

The design of second aids is of minor importance. As a rule, their forms are defined by the purpose they serve. Spatially, the 'functional gaps' that they close are thus also their shaping premise – the empty space determines the object. Second aids, as articles of little complexity, and made mostly of plastic, are attractive to manufacturers. As an object, freed from packaging copy and catalogue descriptions, and from its host object, which would otherwise hint at its purpose, the second aid becomes a mysterious, hermetic sculpture, which further pretends to be 'truly functionalist'.

As additions, all second aids, whether home-made or mass-produced, change the given form or function of an object. In symbiosis with the second aid, the 'host' object is made suitable for the user. The symbiotic relationship is always binding for the second aid, that is, without its partner – for example, the drip-catcher without the coffee pot – it is useless.

The duration of the connection between the second aid and the product may vary from the brief moment of use to an enduring partnership. In principle, the second aid can be removed again from its host without leaving a trace. The 'adapted' object can therefore be returned to its original state at any time.

Only occasionally are second aids, as additions, the heralds of their own integration. This is surprising, considering their claim to be able to perfect the imperfect world of objects. Instead, the 'complementarity claim', and hence the second aid itself, often proves to be an ephemeral fad. Yet the phenomenon, manifesting itself in new ways constantly, remains current.

If we go back far enough, we find that the first acts of civilization were the use of tools, the gaining of power over fire, and the construction of dwellings. Among these the acquisition of power over fire stands out as a quite exceptional achievement, without a prototype; while the other two opened up paths which have ever since been pursued by man, the stimulus towards which is easily imagined. By means of all his tools, man makes his own organs more perfect – both the motor and the sensory – or else removes the obstacles in the way of their activity. Machinery places gigantic power at his disposal which, like his muscles, he can employ in any direction; ships and aircraft have the effect that neither air nor water can prevent his traversing them. With spectacles he corrects the defects of the lens in his own eye; with telescopes he looks at far distances; with the microscope he overcomes the limitations in visibility due to the structure of his retina. With the photographic camera he has created an instrument which registers transitory visual impressions, just as the gramophone does with equally transient auditory ones; both are at bottom materializations of his own power of memory. With the help of the telephone he can hear at distances which even fairy tales would treat as insuperable; writing to begin with was the voice of the absent; dwellings were a substitute for the mother's womb, that first abode, in which he was safe and felt so content, for which he probably yearns ever after.

... Long ago [man] formed an ideal conception of omnipotence and omniscience which he embodied in his gods. Whatever seemed unattainable to his desires – or forbidden to him – he attributed to these gods. One may say, therefore, that these gods were the ideals of his culture. Now he has himself approached very near to realizing this ideal, he has nearly become a god himself. But only, it is true, in the way that ideals are usually realized in the general experience of humanity. Not completely; in some respects not at all, in others only by halves. Man has become a god by means of artificial limbs, so to speak, quite magnificent when equipped with all his accessory organs; but they do not grow on him and they still give him trouble at times. However, he is entitled to console himself with the thought that this evolution will not come to an end in AD 1930. Future ages will produce further great advances in this realm of culture, probably inconceivable now, and will increase man's likeness to a god still more. But with the aim of our study in mind, we will not forget, all the same, that the human being of today is not happy with all his likeness to a god.

Sigmund Freud, *Civilization and Its Discontents*, 1930

Telephone receiver support

Hands-free conversation

It's practically a daily problem in the office: using the telephone while you're making notes, typing on the computer, adding an appointment to your diary, paging through files or brochures – all with one hand, because with the other you have to hold the telephone receiver in the right position next to your ear. How often haven't you pressed the receiver to your ear with a hunched shoulder?

[Der Ideenmarkt, 1994]

Margit Weinberg Staber

Design: ... it's dripping

One day, the paper drip-catcher vanished. The simple white rosette with a hole in the middle didn't exist any more. Inconspicuous and environmentally friendly, one could just put it over the spout of the teapot. As a replacement, the shops selling household goods offered pathetic little sponge rolls, which could be attached to elastic threads pulled around the middle of the pot and secured to the handle with a wire hook. Triple packs in pink, yellow and light green with a plastic butterfly of the same colour on each roll. Aesthetic sensibilities were offended. Undaunted, the pot drips and drips. I wipe away the trickling drops with a paper tissue and think about design. Obviously the paper drip-catcher is not a design product but rather an invention created to conceal unresolved design problems.

Actually, designers are not to be envied for their work. In the eighties, the architects of the postmodern avant-garde began to design coffee pots and teapots. To come up with shapes for everyday household items which had never been seen before appeared virtually impossible. These were more like stylistic finger exercises, as the body of a pot is a three-dimensional object with sculptural characteristics. Form triumphed over function; the Werkbund maxim was inverted. Robert Venturi and Michael Graves joined in, the Italians had Aldo Rossi, and the Italian household-goods manufacturer Alessi was producing luxury objects. In Ettore Sottsass and Alessandro Mendini, Italy already had the progenitors of the new design philosophy. In the hands of the elite, the highly refined style repertoire of the postmodern had an inimitable, elite elegance. There they stood, the crazily mannered pots and jugs. The consequences were predictably awful in a market landscape where innovations are taken over ruthlessly. This over-elaboration turned out to be just as unbearable as the under-elaboration of ossified 'good design'.

However, a few designs managed to penetrate our sense of form in a subtle way. Hermann Gretsch (1895–1950), a man influenced by the Werkbund, was able to turn aesthetic flights of fancy into reliable, useful objects. He worked in the German porcelain industry for decades, and several of his designs are still in production. He maintained: 'When it comes to the shape of the spout, care should be taken that it pours well and does not drip. However, the latter can hardly be avoided.' And this experienced professional added succinctly: 'Drip-catchers, which one hangs around the spout or places under

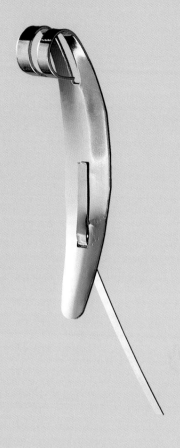

Force field

On the physics of the drip-catcher

It cleverly uses the physical forces that prevail when pouring tea or coffee: gravity tugs the last drop hanging on the spout downwards, the force of adhesion seeks to oppose it – and because of the small mass and relatively large surface area of the drop, this resistance is steady ... but finally fails. Here is a little gadget that craftily employs capillary action to ensure that the force of adhesion triumphs over gravity.

When the pot is set down again the drop is drawn back in, sparing the tablecloth. So, more than thirty years ago, the Westphalian metal-working firm Schulte-Ufer had already solved one of the basic problems of the tea- and coffee-drinking masses.

[Manufactum, catalogue text]

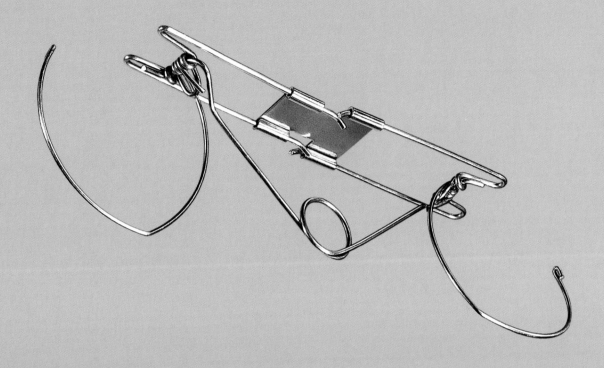

Lid holder

For nearly all pots!

The stainless-steel lid holder is simply attached to the under-
side of the lid. When it's put on the pot, the securing wires
bend together and then spread out again, pressing invisibly
against the inside of the pot. And so the lid holder keeps a
sure grip during pouring.

the base of the pot, are generally not decorative. They should be dispensed with, as the tablecloth will have to be changed frequently for other reasons.' Of course, one does not feel comfortable with the common-sense lessons contained in one of Gretsch's primers from the thirties. The ideals of the Werkbund turned out to be too close to the ideological populism of 'German craftsmanship'. Instead of the theory and philosophy of design, one should perhaps be pursuing the history of design, which could clarify these matters critically.

■ Drop-Stop
Drip-free pouring (EUR. PAT 0 560 777)

Supertop

Body: 100% polystyrene; slider: 100% ABS

1. Stand the carton up with the broadest side of the top facing you.
   Rest the Supertop dispenser with its lid closed on top of the carton,
   from the front left to the back right. Press the dispenser down
   carefully until the two pins touch the carton.

2. With a single movement push the Supertop dispenser through the
   carton, until it locks on to the top securely.

3. Slide the lid open with your thumb and forefinger.

4. The dispenser is now ready to use. Close the lid again after use.

[Paradiso, packaging copy]

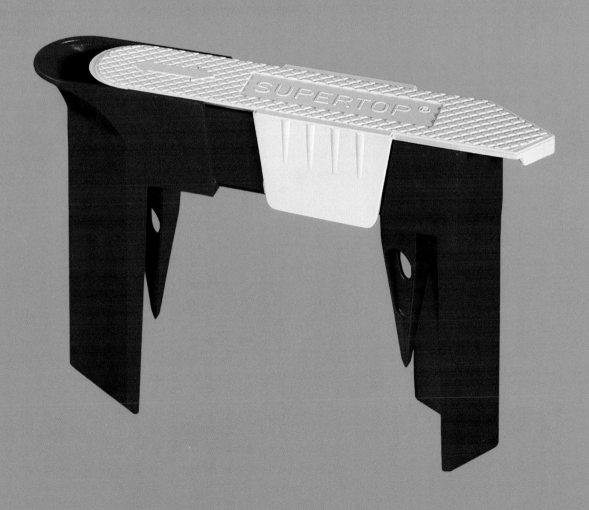

Paper drip-catcher

5 cm diameter

These decorative Duni drip-catchers have many different uses. As well as offering protection against dripping from teapots and coffee pots, they can also be used to stabilize candles in candle holders.

[Duni, packaging copy]

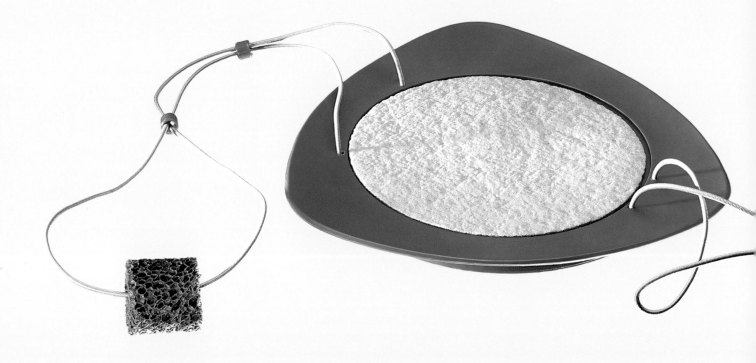

'Neue Form'

Pot coaster with drip-catcher

Bought in East Berlin in 1987. (GDR-Mark 2.20)

But when the spout has a hole …

It was handy, durable, stackable, this GDR caterers' crockery named 'Rationell', made in Colditz in Saxony, and adaptable to every interior – from a hotel to a factory canteen. And as for its distinctive centrepiece 'Portion Pot' (still known familiarly as the 'Mitropa-Pot'), this was, above all, drip-free during pouring. Of course, millions of users had the opposite experience now and then.

Margarete Jahny, the now 77-year-old designer who created 'Rationell' together with Erich Müller at the end of the sixties, remembers it exactly: 'When we were considering the spout and the experiences of other producers, we discovered to our pleasant surprise that the famous Bauscher patent with the hole had expired. And so we wanted to take over this Bauscher trick, which would have cost GDR businesses nothing in foreign currency. But unfortunately nothing came of it. It was decided that unnecessary additional labour would be required in the manufacture of the series. So we fiddled around with the spout until it was drip-free to a large extent even without the little perforation.'

The irony of the story: shortly afterwards, in a German-German countermove, Bauscher profited from Colditz – also thanks to a patent. Erich Müller had invented a new inner shape for the lid of the 'Portion Pot', which made it possible to pour down to the last drop without having to hold the flat cylindrical top. 'Before the particularly lengthy patent procedure had been finalized in the GDR,' Margarete Jahny says with annoyance even today, '"Rationell" was presented with pride to West German sales representatives at the Colditz negotiations stand at the Leipzig Trade Fair, and especially the brilliant solution for the lid. And then in the shortest time Bauscher added it to their own new hotel service – with exactly the same inner shape to the lid, which could never have been mass-produced so quickly in a large GDR firm with its obsolete technology.'

For more about 'Rationell' see Margarete Jahny and Erich Müller in Günter Höhne, *Die Anmut des Rationalen* (Designzentrum Sachsen-Anhalt, Dessau, 1998).

▪ Bauscher patent

Coffee filter anti-kinking device

Keeps filter paper in shape

No more nasty surprises when making coffee. An innovative idea from Fackelmann: the coffee filter anti-kinking device. This smart new household helper prevents the filter paper from caving in when you're making coffee. It is made of stable plastic, designed to suit all tastes and easy to clean. Another advantage: the practical handle allows you to remove it comfortably and cleanly from the filter. Fackelmann's coffee filter anti-kinking device fits all the latest coffee machines.

[Fackelmann, press release]

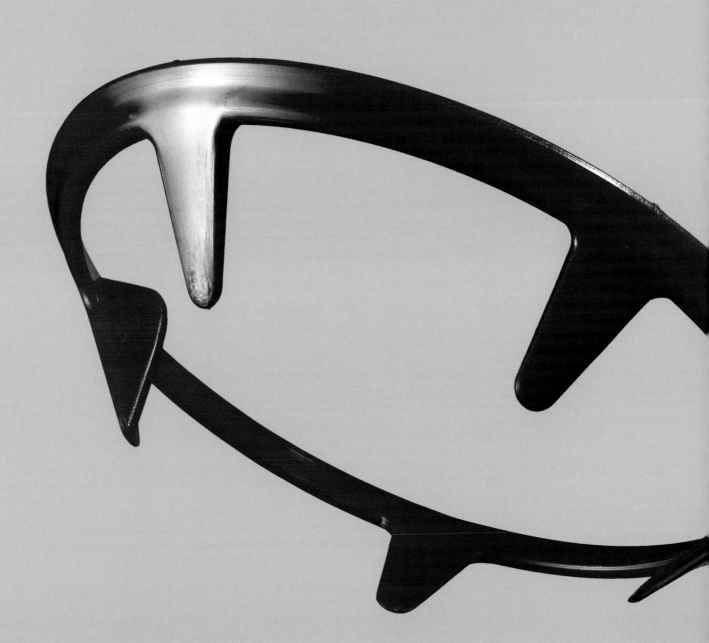

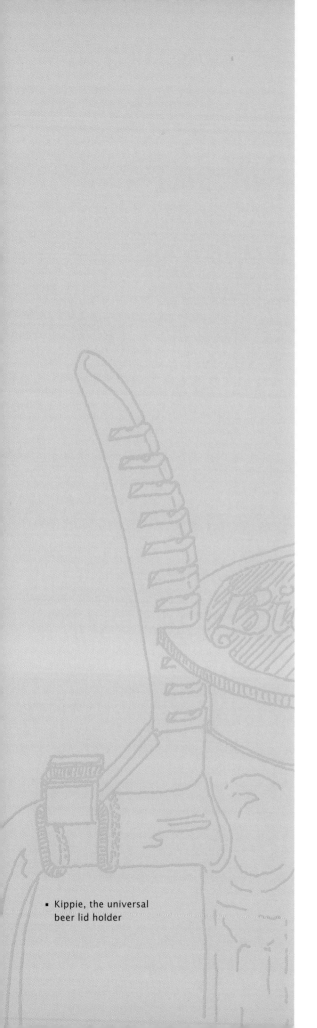

• Kippie, the universal
beer lid holder

Bruno Gruber (59), Olching
Inventor
Door hinge hook
Other inventions: 500

This trained radio mechanic created his first invention at the age of 25. Today he spends 10 per cent of
his time developing new products and 90 per cent
marketing them. He invests an average of about
10 000 Euro in each invention. Although he has often
had to get into debt, he can live off his inventions. In
1998, he was awarded the silver Diesel Medal by the
German Institute of Invention (Deutsches Institut für
Erfindungswesen). He is a member of the German Association of Inventors (Deutscher Erfinder Verband).

Karl Broscheid (52), Königswinter
Core drill entrepreneur
Removable backrests for marquee benches
Other inventions: none

Poor seating on marquee benches prompted his
only invention to date. He has not earned anything
out of it yet, but has already laid out 2 500 Euro.
The 'defects in the use of a product' inspire him to
further inventions.

Siegfried Stölzel (57), Marienheide
Policeman (trained pastry chef)
Spoda – Caravan spoiler with integrated tent
Other inventions: none

He has invested hundreds of hours and 40 000
Euro in his invention. His market-ready product
was introduced at the 'Caravan Salon' in Düsseldorf
in autumn. So far he has only incurred costs, but
he remains optimistic, even though the 'outlay in
time and money' wears him down psychically. 'As
an individual inventor, you walk into walls,' he says.

Doorstop

Freno de puerta – no mas golpes

Found in a hardware store in Majorca.

[Ansima S.A.]

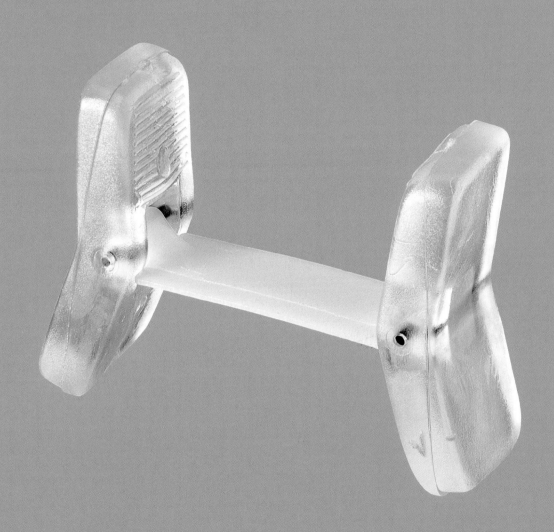

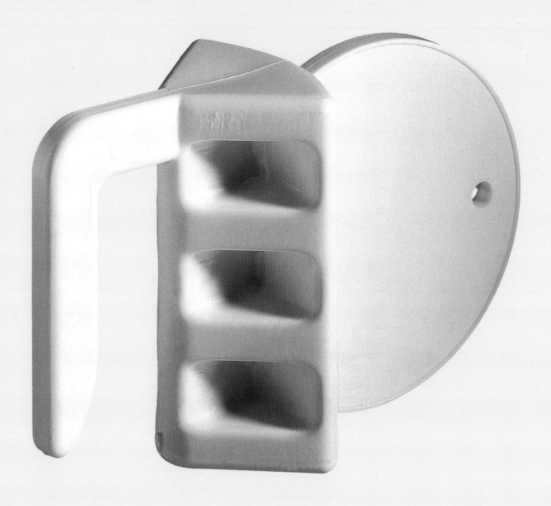

Tür-Klemmi ('Door-Clippo') door catch

Protects children's hands

To use the door catch simply hang it on the hinge of the door. Attach a little loop to the catch, using the specially provided hole, so that when the device is not in use it can be hung somewhere within easy reach. Please note: although our safety devices are made to protect your child, they are no substitute for a parent's vigilance and attention.

[Kess, packaging copy]

Wolfgang Pauser

Things are whole parts

On the philosophy of incompleteness

What is a thing? A thing becomes a thing through its relative isolation from other things, through its apparent being-for-itself, through its containment in itself. It is not a part of another thing, it is not connected, but forms an entity which remains the same despite a change of location or use. In spite of the way in which we take for granted our concept of the thing, by their own definition there are no things in the everyday world. Because most things are tools, whether for work or for play, and as such they are never completely independent but rather doubly connected: to the human body on the one hand and to other tools on the other.

Most things in the everyday world are machines, mainly electrical ones, sometimes driven by fuel. They are connected to cables or pipelines. Does a toaster not become a complete machine only together with the cable and the power station? But this whole machine is still not a thing. This leads the technical philosopher Rudolf Heinz to speak of a 'thing-phantasm'. The idea that there could be a separate, totally disconnected thing is just as unavoidable as it is crazy. For even the simplest tool, such as a hammer, only becomes a tool in combination with the human arm that moves it. In use, it forms a single entity with the human body; to the extent that, conversely, if there is no hammer, the human fist can be used as one. In the use of tools, the boundary between the human body and the world is unclear. When driving, the edge of the car is the boundary of my body. However, if I misuse my fist as a hammer, I distance myself from this part of my body to fend off the pain. I do not then say 'I hurt', I say 'my fist hurts'. Where my own imaginary body boundary is at any time can be described as the thing-phantasm of physical self-interpretation. The need to interpret things as separate entities is a result of our projection of the need for an imaginary self-limitation of the body in the material external world. In doing so, both the body is misunderstood as being disconnected and things are imagined to be disconnected. Whether the projection of the wish for bodily wholeness came before the production of things, or whether, vice versa, things first provided the model for the idea of having a body, cannot be stated. However, humans definitely imagine their own bodies as disconnected, which is why transitionary stages and connections are felt to be embarrassing when they become visible. For example, the serviette is used for the quick removal of things which have half lost their self-boundary and thereby their thingness, while the other half has already entered the juice-world of the body's innards. Half-eaten is disgusting. This also applies to other body openings and connecting places.

In the design of electrical equipment, the thing-phantasm shows itself in the fact that the input leads are seldom accentuated. The cables come out of the appliances at the bottom and are inconspicuously concealed, as if they did not belong to them. The opening of a car's petrol tank also does not stretch greedily towards the petrol pump but disappears bashfully behind a little door.

This thing-world therefore consists of nothing but parts of larger tool combinations, yet serves to represent the symbolic need for separateness, exemplified in relation to the idea of wholeness of a body. Things are parts, which have their own body and are whole, in the sense that people want to have their own, whole body. And people want such a thing-like, whole body all the more because the non-identity of soul and body makes such wholeness impossible from the outset. The thing-phantasm of bodily wholeness is intended to compensate for the non-wholeness of a soul which is already divided by the fact that it can reflect on its own body as an object.

Whereas things can only live up to the thing-phantasm in a fundamental misconception, because they are connected to human bodies and other functionally interrelated things, sculptures are the only things in the sense of the thing-phantasm. They fulfil the desire for the representation of a body boundary as an ideal. They fulfil this desire at the cost of leaving the human world, because they are unwieldy and touching them is forbidden. Only the admiring glance of narcissistic identification may bring them closer to people; the reconnection to the body (for the purposes of its participation in their affliction-free completeness) must not take place physically. Sculptures are as absolute as the thing-phantasm would like things and bodies to be. They are the only real 'things' in the world.

Things on supermarket shelves and in shop windows have a thing-like status similar to that of sculptures for a short time, because they have already escaped the connections to the human and mechanical bodies which made them, have shed all traces of the production work done on them, and have not yet suffered the connections to the body and tool world of the consumers. In this short interval between production and consumption, consumer goods become thing-like,

whole, complete and sculptural. At this stage of being a thing, they are like art works, only accessible to being looked at. As soon as they have been bought and unwrapped, the glorious absolutism of things is over. They start to become things of the past. They are left to their fate of being used and consumed by human bodies, and decay united with them.

From the point of view of sculptural, absolute thingness, the everyday reality of an industrial manufacturing consumer society can be understood as follows: work is the process which disconnects things from productive human bodies ('alienation') so that – in the shop – before they are reconnected through consumption, in the realm of possibilities of the delayed exchange, they possess that strangeness which awakens a desire for them that is beyond any useful purpose they might have. Alienation promotes the phantasmagorical thing-seal underlining the fetish character of the goods and the unconsciousness of the motives of the producer. For the sake of thingness, things become goods through exchange. The alienation of the goods serves the constitution of the object, and it is only the objectness, which becomes clear in the thing form, which elicits in consumers the stirring of desire. What is disappointing in the act of consumption is that the acquired thing loses its sculptural thing character when it is connected to the context of its use by the consumer body which consumes and uses it. The goods lose their shine in the shabbiness of being used. The alienation only disappoints because it awakens a flicker of hope for narcissistic identification with an absolute thing-like object which can never be fulfilled in the act of consumption. This painful disappointment caused by the industrial presentation of thing-like goods can only be opposed by creating sculptures. Sculptures escape the fate of disappointing consumption. The fact that they cannot be used keeps the aura of goods about them forever.

The counter-parts to the sculptures that outdo the thing-world are the second aids, the sub-things, the adapters and protective coverings and additions. They are easily missed by conscious awareness because they are concerned with transitions. They are coy parts, totally lacking in wholeness. In contrast to proper things, which at least postulate independence for themselves, the supplementary things not only betray their miserable status of unwholeness but also create awareness of the wholeness-drama of things in an irksome way. Second aids blow the whistle on the embarrassing trade secret of thing narcissism.

Their users do not want to be seen in public with them. They are symptoms, undesired side effects of the sacrifice to functionality rendered by the producers of things to the thing-phantasm. Like a mirror image of the desire which springs from narcissistic identification with thing wholeness, the ugliness of second aids shows itself in the expression of a fundamental lack. From a psychoanalytical point of view, the thing as such has a phallic quality, while the second aids symbolize the opposite, the lack of wholeness. Adding to the wholeness of things is embarrassing for exactly this reason.

Adapters appear shabby, even when they are new. And it does not matter how clean they are, they still seem to befoul the order of things. When guests visit, one prefers to do without the teapot's drip-catcher. One does not want to run the risk that it might not work on important occasions. The fact that second aids are often intended to prevent or hide shabbiness does not help them. When they themselves can be seen, shabbiness becomes more clearly evident as a problem than it would be with regard to any sign of wear and tear, which, as the patina of things, cannot be removed, but, on the contrary, is proof of generosity in dealing with them. By contrast, second aids are petty, they indicate exaggerated fear and thriftiness, worries about the stability and efficiency of the thing boundary. They betray the fact that their users are ready to sacrifice narcissistic identification with themselves and, symptomatically, with their things for a small practical advantage.

The typical user of second aids does not just sacrifice his positive self-image, that is, the expectation of being looked at with love, for the practical. This version is his rationalization. Behind this he hides the real purpose of second aids – self-hate, accepted castration, the successful renunciation of wanting to be loved, the need to show the narcissistic void in a symptom. The fan of the all-too-practical tells others: 'Like my things I may not be beautiful, but instead I'm sensible!' However, he is the only one who benefits from this good sense.

The second aid shows that its user has given up wanting to fulfil his narcissistic need to be loved via the arduous route of libidinous recognition from other people. Instead, the 'practical person' prefers to enjoy immediately his own small advantage, the smallest of advantages. He is an enjoyer of himself, calls it 'comfort', and apparently no longer needs communication and the dialectics of recognition for his well-being. Disappointed at being insufficiently admired as an object, he has made his narcissism private but made the subjectivism of his bodily sensitivities absolute. Things become a little like artificial limbs to social-aesthetic autists; the standard for judging them is now only one's own body feelings, against which the pleasure of possible guests and observers counts for little.

As a result, things must follow the attitude of giving up object status. The second aid industry serves the frustrated philistine with symbols of his demonstrative lack of vanity. These symbols always give the appearance of being especially practical and sensible. And it is good that they do, because undisguised their meaning would be unbearable.

- Door-mounted hooks
- Key fastener
- NUK doorstop
- Door-mounted coat rack
- Multihook
- Tope Amortiguador
- Draught stopper
- Doorstop
- Doorknob cover
- Window clip
- Doorknob cover
- Rubber window stopper

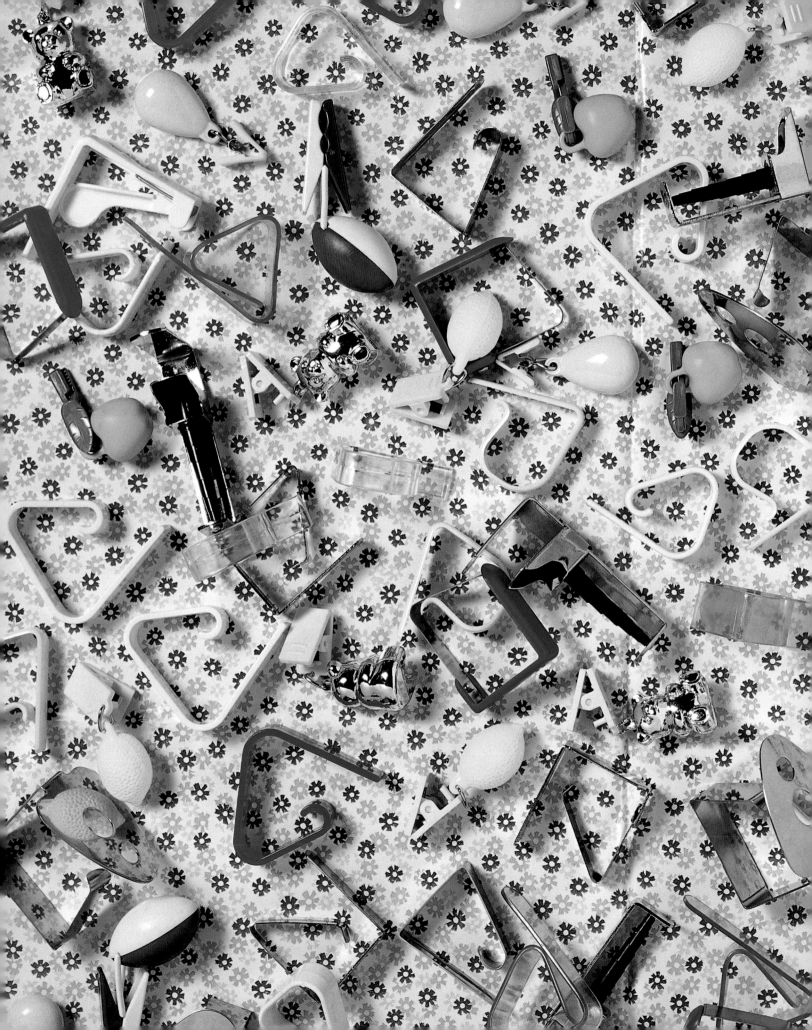

Suckerfish

Size isn't everything

For countless nameless drip-catchers and table-cloths, room fountains and window clips, that legendary encounter between umbrella and sewing machine on a Parisian dissecting table is etched, a symbol of unattainable emancipation, on to their obscure bodies. Not for them an independent existence. They adorn, perfect and complete that which is already there. Their existence depends on objects which do not depend on them. It's an unequal relationship. However, in the eyes of their owners, these second aids add both functional and aesthetic value. Their worth is priceless. They effortlessly inhabit a world full of perfect, beautiful and emanative things, lending each a personal signature.

In sensuously opulent fashion, the drip-catcher – one of the most popular symbiotic gadgets around, and nothing without a pot – reveals just what its owner feels is lacking in the design: a visual guarantee of function. This attack on the 'pure form' by the tactile and the trivial transforms the abstract standard into a personal declaration of taste. So what exactly is happening? Doesn't each foreign body – each drip-catcher – compromise the designer's claim to perfection?

Of course, the coffee firmament is full of pots, from which it rains in very different ways. In other words, the market is already saturated with a vast spectrum of concrete answers to individual needs, both real and fictitious. Nevertheless, no amount of improvement or differentiation has managed to make the second aids superfluous. And that's hardly surprising, since their first priority is not to attack the shape of the object, but rather its identity-bestowing rhetoric. They respect neither the autonomy of things, nor the designer's aesthetic artistry.

The subversive energy of these little second aids should inspire us to consider the sense and purpose of objectification. We see ourselves reflected in the things we design or acquire. In this way, the products with which we surround ourselves are constantly defining our identity. It remains to be seen whether this subject-object arrangement will remain a significant element in the constitution of identity in the future.

Many a heated debate has already taken place concerning the potential effects of media extension on the human as an individual. 'Within the realm of communication, things, people and looks are in a continual state of virtual contact, never really touching, the proximity or distance of the other echoing the relationship of the body to its surroundings.' Virtual worlds – according to Jean Baudrillard – open a dimension, 'which no longer belongs to humans; an eccentric dimension, of the depolarization of space and the dissolution of bodily form.'[1] In the face of a prognosticated breakdown of relationships as we know them, we must ask what representative roles things are likely to play in future. We are currently witnessing

- Tablecloth clips
- Tablecloth bobbles
- Tablecloth weights

a high-speed turnover in group-specific and individual characteristics. This is particularly noticeable among the young. These days, the identity bestowed by certain material attributes is destined to be temporary. That the certainty of the distinctive, the personal and the incongruous is sought, yet not wanted on a permanent basis, is not confined to teenagers. Our desire, or more correctly, our craving for the exclusive and individual has spawned the inflation of design in the fleeting guise of objects. Thus emanative objects compensate us for feelings of loss engendered by the insensate and incorporeal world of the global information network.

Until now, designers have applauded this development, switching their attention to the differentiation of things. However, those who attempt to foil this increase in fickle consumer behaviour with design diversity alone will soon find themselves suffering from aesthetic burnout. In the long run, object-orientated design can no longer guarantee innovative flexibility. But accepting mutability and mobility as cultural phenomena also means improving the design of open systems, designing artefacts capable of creating and adapting to a variety of contexts. As a result, 'use cannot be separated from design and creation: the design determines what might be, it is alternative reality …'[2]

One aspect of design practice worth taking seriously is the rediscovery of object universality. A table is as much for reading and writing as it is for eating and playing. It may be a sober desk that with the simple addition of a tablecloth becomes a dining table. More flexibility is created by using 'symbiotic' elements than by purchasing and using function-specific variants of 'the table'. And that's not all. It also makes huge ecological sense. This has nothing to do with utilitarian regression, or the priggish promotion of an ascetic lifestyle. On the contrary, it is the de-individualization of objects that opens them to individualization: as design variables in the individual

determination of living environments. That's when little symbiotic gadgets really come into their own; like suckerfish, they dock on to unspecific everyday items, altering function, endowing an aura of aesthetic individualism – and leaving their 'host' just as quickly as they arrive.

Universal, semantically neutral objects are increasingly in demand in places where dynamic structures necessitate frequent changes in ownership: in the world of work. Its modern-day emblem is the computer. The computer is the perfect example of a new kind of object, where functional and semantically distinct design intentions are destined to fail. The computer has no fixed job description. Its plastic shell remains unchanged, regardless of its range of functions and any number of potential users. It draws no distinction between bookkeeper and board member. A symbol of modernity and technological expertise, the computer remains abstract. As with other media technologies, the widespread availability of computers contributes to the 'trivialization of uniqueness' (Abraham Moles). This basically means that any attempt to lend aesthetic significance to these appliances, neutral in terms of location, time and subject, becomes a design curiosity. The simple fact that software wears out more quickly than a computer's outer shell throws any design premise focusing solely on the function of an object into doubt. Today, computers are to be found on every desk. They are bound into a spatial context that strives by aesthetic means to lend definition to location, desk and user. Here we see a (potential) collision of two models concerned with the organization of things: the one, based on a traditional division of labour, deals with individual objects; the other, the computer model, can only be appreciated per se as a series of processes.

That the functions of a computer do not determine its appearance is more than just a succinct observation. Rather, the discontinuity between inner workings and outer shell should be regarded as an indication of an epochal break with convention. The 'new' interfaces cannot be defined using cogitative norms of opposition – near and far, culture and nature, object and subject, mind and matter, etc. The computer is a paradigm of boundlessness. It synchronizes spaces separated by geographical distance, transactions, and information. It brings 'immediacy ... to the mechanical world. ... The instant synchronization of numerous transactions signifies the end for the mechanical enumeration of transactions in linear succession.'[3] And thus the time-space continuum as a structure-giving element loses its validity. McLuhan prognosticates the dissolution of 'linear succession' in the organization of our civilization, replacing it with a 'holistic sphere of experience ..., where all

kinds of impressions and experiences will be exchanged and translated ...'[4] Following McLuhan's train of thought, people and objects will soon become factors of a virtual whole, unrestricted by adherence to any hierarchical system of organization. Objects must therefore be increasingly examined according to their ability to be combined. The more specific their aesthetic and functional features, the harder it will be to integrate them into ever-changing contexts. So it is probably wise to leave the job of object individualization to the second aids. The chance encounter of the umbrella and the sewing machine may well have been a turning point for the emancipation of things – the dissecting table, on the other hand, was far from being a good omen.

[1] Jean Baudrillard, 'Videowelt und fraktales Subjekt', in Jean Baudrillard, Hannes Böhringer, Vilém Flusser, Heinz von Foerster, Friedrich Kittler and Peter Weibel, *Philosophien der neuen Technologien* (Ars Electronica, Berlin, 1989), p. 122.

[2] Bernd Meurer, 'Die Zukunft des Raums', in *Die Zukunft des Raums* (Campus Verlag, Frankfurt/New York, 1994).

[3] Marshall McLuhan, *Die magischen Kanäle [Understanding Media]*, 2nd expanded edition (Verlag der Kunst, Dresden/Basel, 1995), p. 524.

[4] ibid., p. 23.

Suckerfish

(Echeneidae family)
Remora remora,
Max. length 64 cm

Suckerfish attach by means of a sucking disk to large sea creatures such as sharks, bony fish, and turtles, allowing themselves to be 'transported' through the water, often over large distances. They feed off tiny, parasitic crustaceans found on the skin of their 'transporters'.

[Steinbach's Guide to Saltwater Fish]

Enquiries at Fackelmann

Willi Aichert (Fackelmann Design Department), Arzu Alagöz (Fackelmann Product Management)

Mr Aichert, do you have a coffee filter anti-kinking device in your own home?

Aichert Of course. To check whether it really works.

How did the idea of the coffee filter anti-kinking device come about? We would have thought that hardly anyone makes their coffee in this traditional way any more.

Alagöz It was like this. Somebody sent in the idea. Mr Fackelmann said, 'This is our kind of thing!' We in the Marketing Department thought ... well, to be honest, we weren't 100 per cent behind it. But Mr Fackelmann – it's one of his strong points – has a feel for such products, like the Ballermann drinking straw. He simply felt, 'I've got to have it!' And, in fact, the turnover has been very good. As far as the anti-kinking device is concerned, we said, okay, it's something you could sell, but only with the right packaging and as a secondary line. Now it's displayed all over the place, wherever coffee is available. Right by the coffee shelves. Which automatically stimulates impulse buying.

In your Design Department, how do you get from idea to mass product?

Aichert The coffee filter anti-kinking device reached us from Marketing as a concrete proposal. We then worked on making it as cheap and simple to produce as possible. A fundamental improvement was the addition of a handle, which hadn't been provided for in the original design. On the basis of a few sketches we built a model, and then after some calculations and production decisions we came up with a scale drawing. Clarifying the sales

appeal of the item, through its value and usefulness, required a combination of graphic design and cardboard packaging design. In the case of the anti-kinking device, it took about two days to come up with the design, the model and the packaging. And ten to twelve weeks to reach the finished product. Market research or product testing wasn't really an issue.

Does your company have a name for the products we call 'second aids'?

Alagöz Not really. I call them little problem solvers, and Mr Aichert has his own term for them.

And how successful is a well-marketed second aid?

Alagöz The real winners sell hundreds of thousands every year.

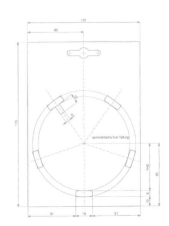

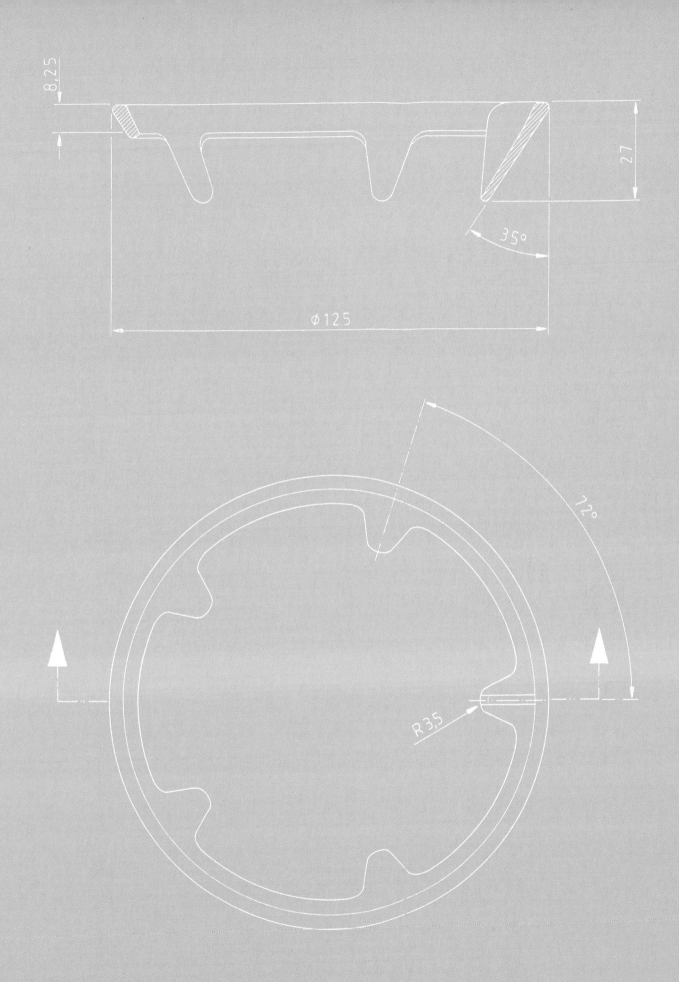

This interview with Udo Engelke (Marketing Manager, Thomashilfen) was conducted by Andrea Vilter, Jörg Adam and Dominik Harborth at the Academy Schloss Solitude, Stuttgart, on 13 January 2000.

Things have to adapt

On the 'helping hand' and other assistive devices

Mr Engelke, it's interesting that in your field there is a name for the things we call 'second aids'. In most areas, such as household goods or car accessories, these items are acknowledged yet have no collective name. By contrast, you employ an official term, which seems very apt, by the way: assistive devices. If one examines these items, they all have one thing in common. They assist in the use of everyday objects, which would otherwise no longer be usable for certain people. It's not that the objects have suddenly become unsuitable, but rather that the people themselves have been disabled, and so a gap suddenly opens up, which can be closed by a prosthesis. If I lose an arm, I can acquire a prosthetic one, at great expense. By contrast, the assistive devices function as product prostheses. They allow me to make the things around me usable again with only one arm. For instance, I might attach a food guard to the rim of my plate, or screw a knob to the steering wheel of my car, so that I can turn it with one hand.

Engelke Quite right. Any adaptation to the disability of a particular user may be classified as an assistive device. A directory of such items exists, in which thirty different product groups are divided into various categories according to their application – from bathing aids and hearing aids right through to wheelchairs. These categories were originally defined by specialists in terms of specific product-related criteria. In the meantime, this has become an extremely complex issue – and with good cause. It's in all of our interests to prevent the market being swamped by shoddy merchandise. We just have to see to it that the bureaucracy doesn't produce any howlers.

With whom does Thomashilfen do business? Do you approach medical suppliers? Is it possible to place a direct order?

Engelke It works like this: there are the manufacturers, the retailers, the public institutions, and the health authorities. We approach both therapists and retailers about products which in the event will be paid for by a third party – either the health authority, the health insurance company, or another institution, such as the employment office or social services. An estimate reflecting the needs of the patient is submitted to the relevant body by the medical supplier. If approved, this body finances the purchase of the product, which we then deliver to the retailer in question. As far as invoicing is concerned, Thomashilfen has no direct contact with the patient. It's the retailer who is recognized by the health authority as the health care provider, and it's therefore up to the retailer to deliver the items and provide any necessary advice and aftercare. That's one reason why we only do business with specialist medical suppliers.

Are the products you offer all covered by state health insurance, or are there exceptions?

Engelke There's no fixed percentage. However, everything contained in the children's rehab catalogue, for instance, is covered. And if we take a look at 'Everyday Care', you'll see that many articles for the care of the elderly are given a particular item number. Number 02, for example, denotes the assistive devices category. This number shows whether a product is covered by the health authority. Of course, the necessary symptoms must be present. Some kind of disability must exist. You can't just say, 'These "helping hand" reachers are great, I want one.' And of course there are also items that are in the process of being approved. Sometimes it can take seven to eight months before a product makes it into the directory. First we submit the application, then the product is tested against a whole catalogue of criteria, and while this is going on we're given a temporary six-figure number for the article. When the last four numbers are also there, it means the product has been incorporated into the directory of assistive devices.

But you can also buy some of these products in the high street. We found the 'helping hand', for example, in a shop calling itself something like 'One thousand humorous gift ideas for the old, the disabled and the left-handed'. It certainly wasn't a medical supplier, more a mixture of trendy lifestyle accessories and household goods. We found several articles that we recognized from your catalogue. They were being sold to people for an arm and a leg, apparently on the strength of their functional appeal, since no one seemed to exhibit any clinical symptoms. Quite apart from the health authorities, there would therefore seem to be a ready market for such products.

Engelke Let's look at the reasons. As I've already said, medical suppliers accept the role of health care provider in order to be able to bill the health authority. Of course, there are many companies that are slowly discovering the rehab sector. Mail-order companies are devoting themselves increasingly to 'healthy living', 'well-being', or 'wellness' – to use the American term. Everyone's very conscious of the age pyramid right now. There's a huge market out there, they tell themselves, and we should take a look at what products already exist for this age group. It's really hardly surprising that the emphasis on design and appearance in our sector is growing.

Does Thomashilfen employ any designers?

Engelke Of course, we have a couple of designers, but we think it's more important that we employ people who enter the field as ergotherapists or physiotherapists. There's not a single person in

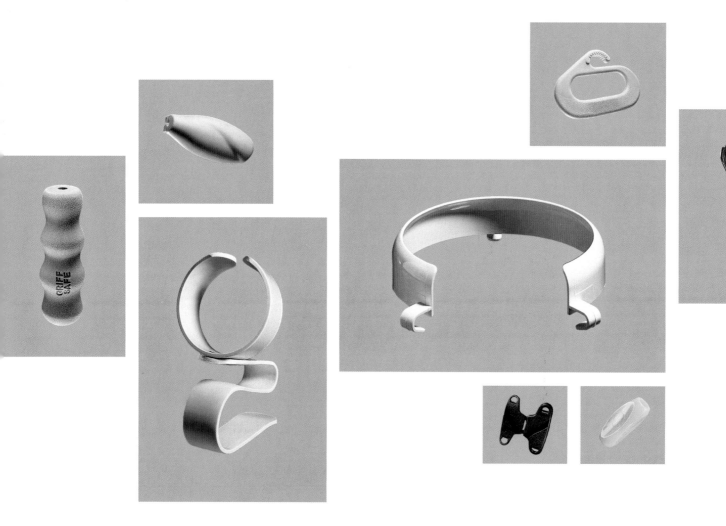

Cutlery handle ▪ Glass holder ▪ Cutlery holder ▪ Food guard ▪ Shopping bag carrier ▪ Key holder ▪ Ergonomic writing grip ▪ Key turner

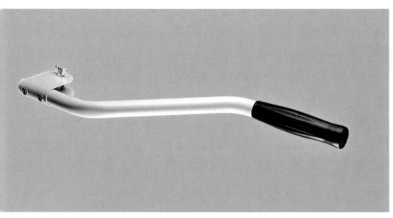

Assistive devices

The Medical Review Board catalogue

Assistive devices restore some independence to the lives of people who, as a result of illness or disability, can no longer use objects and appliances in their unchanged form. Thanks to assistive technology, appliances and objects essential to everyday living and tasks associated with fulfilling the basic human needs are once more within reach.

Everyday items are not covered by insurance, even if specially designed for people with disabilities. This includes articles for general use, which are normally used by more than one person, or are found in the average household. Also excluded are items used in the preparation or consumption of food, such as chopping boards, electric knives, electric tin openers, pots, crockery, etc.

Door handle lever ▪ Tap turners ▪ Cane holder with trouser-pocket clip ▪ Cane holder ▪ Cane holder ▪ Ice cleat attachment for cane

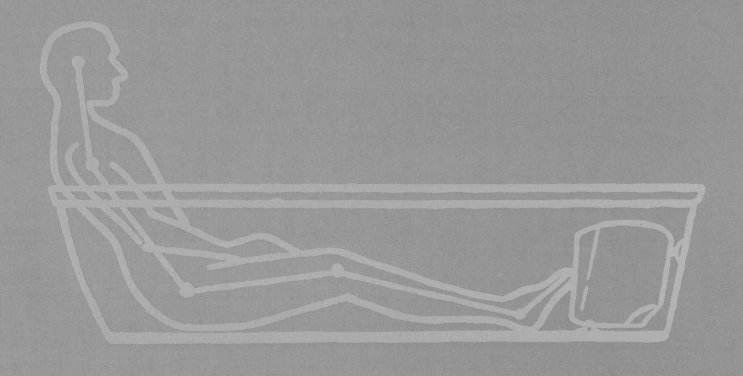

Bath shortener

Safety in the bath, non-scratch

Shorter people can now use the bath with comfort and safety.
The hygienic white plastic bath shortener is placed at the
foot of the bath to prevent slipping down. Four large suckers
hold the bath shortener in place but can be easily removed.

[Meyra, packaging copy]

our team of sales representatives who doesn't have a medical background. That's also why the health authorities wouldn't dream of entering into an agreement with a mail-order company. Certain qualified personnel, let's say an orthopaedic technician, must be on hand to provide service and aftercare – and that's something a mail-order company is unable to do. But, of course, it's also in the interests of the health authorities that people – especially the elderly – are able to buy rehab products by mail order. It would never enter their heads to apply to the health authority for such things. So they end up footing the bill themselves. Which in turn means that a need is met without the health authority having to pay.

And what about this key turner here, is that regarded unequivocally as an assistive device?

Engelke No. You see, it doesn't have an item number. There are products we don't succeed in registering. As a private company, we're not always able to explain the necessity of an item to those making the final decision. For people who suffer from certain rheumatic diseases, this key turner would be a great help. But if you're not permitted to take part in the meetings of the Medical Review Board, which is responsible for formulating product definitions, it's impossible to argue plausibly for the inclusion of a product. Some items simply don't make it into the catalogue, which also means they're not automatically covered by insurance. These are cases where the discretion of the individual clerk comes into play. If the clerk considers an item appropriate for a particular patient, he or she is at liberty to approve its issue as a special case. Understandably, the health authorities are loath to establish a general rule. Why? Because then the whole of Germany will be saying, 'I need a key turner.' It's true, people who come into medical suppliers often display the classic attitude to health insurance: 'If I need something, then someone else should pay for it. What about a "helping hand", I desperately need one of those. Is it covered by insurance? Oh, it's not? Well, maybe I don't

need one after all. Of course, if someone else is going to pay, there's a lot here I like and a lot I could find a use for. But if I'm going to have to stump up myself, then I'm not that interested.' Which is why many articles are simply classified by the Medical Review Board – under contract to the major health authorities – as ordinary, everyday items, to avoid the situation where the authorities are obliged to finance such things for everyone. Take glasses, for instance. Years ago, nobody wore glasses. Now they've become a fashion accessory and the health authorities have reacted by taking them off the list.

So it seems that the question of whether or not I can get something I want on insurance is governed largely by the item's image. The more attractive and commonplace these everyday items of assistive technology are in their design, the greater the conflict when assessing whether the product is only suitable for a person with a disability, or for others as well. If this key turner were made of dull, light-grey rubber, but still did the same job, its appeal would be so minimal that there wouldn't be this confusion between those who are really needy and those who say, 'Actually, I'm also interested in one of these.' The fact that these objects are all very attractive surely encourages this phenomenon. People are bound to view such products as ordinary consumer goods. You want something because you like it, because it looks good. By contrast, this toilet-seat cushion is unattractive. You're only going to want this if you've got a real medical problem.

Engelke There's also a question of perception. In the USA, I don't think it would be a problem to walk out of the supermarket with one of those under your arm, whereas here you'd definitely want a bag. It's basically taboo that certain medical conditions – too much pressure around the coccyx, or whatever – require toilet seats made of something other than plastic. But in the USA, it wouldn't be a problem. People there are far more relaxed about such things. We Germans on the other hand much prefer to order that kind of product from a catalogue, hoping it will eventually arrive by post and that we won't be forced to go to a medical supplier.

These products here seem to come from the USA and England. Is Thomashilfen primarily a sales partner as far as such products are concerned?

Engelke Just because something comes from the USA doesn't necessarily mean it was produced there. Sometimes we have no idea where the items come from, or whether they were originally classic consumer goods that have been assimilated into the assistive technology sector. I'm sure the weirdest stories exist as to how these things were invented.

So you believe that some products are 'normal' things that have been discovered by the rehab sector?

Engelke Yes.

Or the other way round, in the case of the invalid's crank handle. That's the old name for the knob you fit to a car's steering wheel so that you can turn it with one hand. Now this product – in imitation burlwood – is in all the mail-order catalogues for car accessories, and suddenly every driver wants one. Of course, the small print states that you have to be suffering from an appropriate medical complaint to be permitted to use one. Nevertheless, it's made a total transition into the world of everyday products for so-called healthy individuals.

A question about the founding of the company: your brochure states that the idea for the business was born of personal experience?

Engelke That's right. Originally, some sixty years ago, the founder Karl Thomas set up a company called 'Thomas Sitz- und Liegemöbel'. When his wife contracted a wasting disease at the beginning of the seventies, he said to himself, 'We already have

a lot of business contacts, particularly in Scandinavia, I'll ask them if they know any special products which might be of help.' It's important to realize that at the time the Scandinavian countries led the field in the provision of assistive devices. Karl Thomas actually found a lot of ideas and products to help ease his wife's condition – unfortunately only for a short period, as she died just a couple of years later. After a period of reflection, he said to himself, 'I can't be the only person in Germany to have had this problem.' And so, although he was already over sixty, he founded another company – Thomashilfen.

We've discovered that many of these second aids or assistive devices, as you call them, have their origins in personal stories of this kind. Someone is accustomed to using an object in a certain way, suddenly can't for whatever reason, has to find a way around the problem and then, out of the blue, gets creative. Sometimes they even improvise something to make up for a product's shortcomings and approach a manufacturer, while others are talented enough to produce a prototype of the improved design.

Engelke That's certainly true of many products. In the course of a year, we get quite a lot of letters from 'tinkerers'. They write to us full of the solution they've come up with for this or that problem, for themselves or their wife. Some of them even have a degree in engineering or the like. They certainly have an idea of how to go about making such things, so they just get on with it and develop the item in the workshop at home. They're delighted with the finished result, so it's only natural they want to show it to someone. They have a lot in common with Karl Thomas. They too think, 'We're not the only ones with this problem.' However, the crunch comes when you want to start producing such an item. We're actually talking very small quantities. You try finding a company in Germany that's prepared to make, say, a special reacher which turns to the left. Who's going to do it? Hardly anyone. Because the first thing they'll want to know is how many hours of machining will that mean for my production facility, how much lead time will be required, etc., etc. At that point, most people just give up and forget about it, convinced it would never have been worth it!

But are some of the things at least interesting?

Engelke Sure, it's just that we can't follow up on most of them. In the sixteen years I've been with the company, we've developed maybe two or three items. Things like special card holders or a gadget to help pull up tights. But lots of these products are also incredibly specific. So then you have to ask yourself how much energy you're willing to expend trying to get an item into the assistive device register. Those are difficult times, when you wonder who actually benefits and whether you'll really be doing a lot of people a favour. And of course you also have to consider the business side. How much energy should you devote to an area already served by a large number of products, all needing a considerable amount of specialist attention and further development themselves?

In what quantities do you sell your products?

Engelke The problem with the rehab sector is that no one really keeps a record of numbers. It's hard enough to get an idea of how many people currently use wheelchairs in Germany. In the product sector targeting the elderly, however, we have only a very few items which sell in their thousands. That's another reason why many companies maintain it makes no sense to manufacture the items themselves. You're happy if you can find a supplier to keep your own customers supplied. But the quantities you manage to shift are really very small.

Most of the packaging displays the name of the supplier, rather than that of Thomashilfen.

Engelke It simply makes more sense from a commercial point of view. We're quite open about it. Of course, we realize the medical suppliers might try and establish direct contact with the manufacturers. But then they would have to organize the transatlantic shipping themselves. We take a certain risk because we know how our retail partners tend to think. If we were keen on having our own packaging or a Thomashilfen label or whatever, it would still have to be commercially viable for us to go ahead. But because of the negligible quantities involved, it's simply not worth a large investment.

A final question about your own career: how did you end up at Thomashilfen?

Engelke It was Karl Thomas actually. We're neighbours. He asked me what I wanted to do after my military service and I said, 'That's a very good question.' And then it just happened. I'm the last person with a business qualification to have been employed by the company ... and that was sixteen years ago.

A. W. FABER.

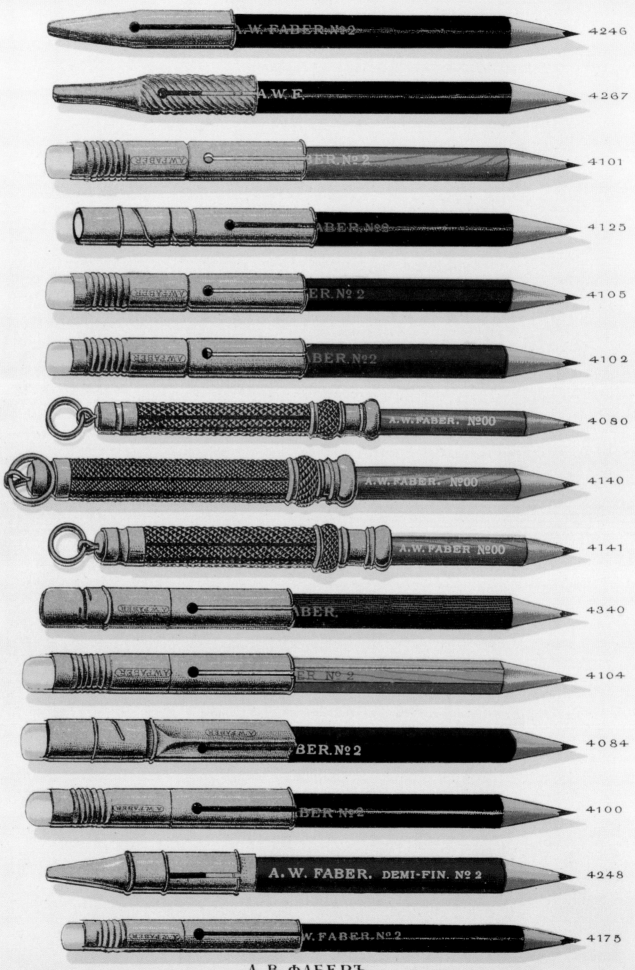

4246

4267

4101

4125

4105

4102

4080

4140

4141

4340

4104

4084

4100

4248

4175

А. В. ФАБЕРЪ.

Bernhard Wördehoff

The pencil extender When the stub still had a future

The pencil has withstood every new wave of technological innovation. Not even that whimsical by-product of space research, the ballpoint pen, which enabled mankind to make notes above his head in zero gravity (something he'd been desperate to do for many years), was able to make much of an impact.

The lead pencil, so-called though it doesn't contain any lead at all (it's crystallized carbon that makes its mark), enjoys a fruitful existence, with seven billion pencils being produced every year. What for? And why so many? These are questions that have exercised Walther Kiaulehn: 'It's difficult to decide whether the pencil is one of life's basic necessities or whether it simply has sentimental appeal. One thing, however, is certain. The pencil will always be an essential piece of equipment. Judging by the quantity of pencils in circulation and the untold numbers which roll off production lines every day, the human race really must have an awful lot to write down, which, were it ever without a pencil, it might be in danger of forgetting.' A considerable proportion of the pencils produced remain unused (somewhere in the region of 20 to 25 per cent). And that's ignoring all the pencils that go missing from offices, forever to remain an unknown quantity. This figure also fails to take into account another aspect which would no doubt make a significant difference to the final tally – the global custom, once especially favoured by the Soviet Union, of lending a conference the necessary gravitas by laying a sharpened pencil on the desk of each individual delegate. Not to be used, you understand, but as a keepsake. How else do you account for an annual production of seven billion pencils?

But we're not really interested in the use or otherwise of the pencil, or its decline into prestigious 'memento-dom'; what concerns us is the humble pencil stub and the poignant question: 'What has become of the pencil stub nowadays, once fated to write until it could write no more – for the good of the economy – thanks to the benevolence of the pencil extender?'

This metal sleeve, a short and simple construct between four and a half and twelve centimetres long, slipped over the end of the stub, rendering it long enough again to write with and comfortable to use. A clever little metal ring prevented the sleeve from slipping off the stub. Our throwaway society has sounded the death knell for an idea as simple and refined as the pencil extender. We honour the memory of its sensible practicality.

▪ Faber-Castell
pencil extenders

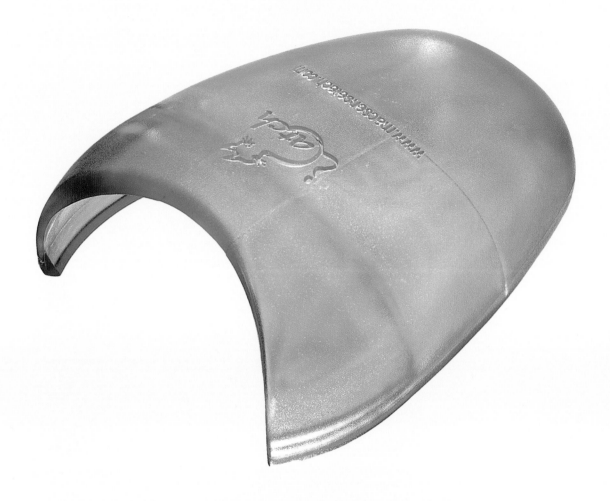

iCatch

patent pending

Stop hand cramps and repetitive strain injury with the new MacSense
iCatch Mouse Adapter. This unit transforms your iMac mouse into an
ergonomically-sound peripheral.

   The iCatch simply snaps onto your iMac mouse, providing you
with the comfortable shape that molds to the natural contours of your
hand. Protect your hands from the pain before it starts with the new
iCatch Mouse Adapter.

[MacSense, packaging copy]

The iCatch story

Phillip Chang, vice-president of MacSense Connectivity Inc., attributes the idea for the iCatch to his daughter who noticed his obvious 'big-hands' handicap when playing games on their iMac. She suggested he strap something on the mouse to make it bigger. iCatch was born.

The MacSense team of engineers consulted with ergonomists to develop a product with the shape, style, and feel of a standard mouse while retaining the traditional Macintosh ease of use.

MacSense advertisement

What the critics are saying about the iMac mouse Arguments for the iCatch

The new iMac computer has debuted to rave reviews from just about all of the Mac publications that have written about it, single-handedly giving Apple an advantage in the battle of the PCs. The only harsh words that have surfaced regarding the new computer were pointed at that squashed-circle of a mouse. Some ergonomists have said the futuristic-looking mouse design placed too much emphasis on aesthetics instead of feel. Dr Alan Hedge told the 'San Jose Mercury News' this compromise could eventually lead to repetitive strain injury in the hands and wrists of users who work a lot. 'MacWorld magazine' and 'San Jose Mercury News' had this to say:

If you're just looking for a better iMac mouse, consider the iCatch. The device snaps on to the round mouse, making it easier to handle while retaining the distinctive iMac style.

MacWorld magazine

Because its size and shape make it difficult to orient, there's a risk users will grip the iMac's mouse tightly, forcing their hands into a stiff claw, according to four ergonomists. Over time, that extra pressure could increase the risk of developing carpal tunnel syndrome, a disease marked by pain in the wrist and small muscles of the hand.

San Jose Mercury News – Amy Doan, 1998

The iMac's translucent keyboard offers good key response and a solid feel. Alas, the same can't be said of the iMac's mouse, where style has won out over substance. Its small form factor makes it difficult to hold comfortably, and because the mouse lacks the oblong shape of a standard mouse, it easily gets turned around.

MacWorld magazine – Andrew Gore, 1998

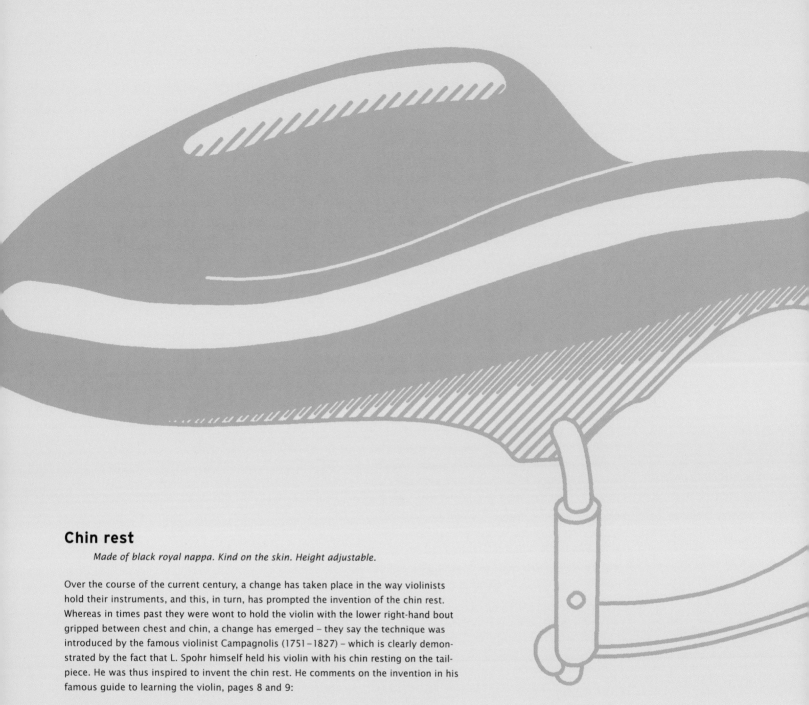

Chin rest

Made of black royal nappa. Kind on the skin. Height adjustable.

Over the course of the current century, a change has taken place in the way violinists
hold their instruments, and this, in turn, has prompted the invention of the chin rest.
Whereas in times past they were wont to hold the violin with the lower right-hand bout
gripped between chest and chin, a change has emerged – they say the technique was
introduced by the famous violinist Campagnolis (1751–1827) – which is clearly demonstrated by the fact that L. Spohr himself held his violin with his chin resting on the tailpiece. He was thus inspired to invent the chin rest. He comments on the invention in his
famous guide to learning the violin, pages 8 and 9:

'The new playing technique, in which the left hand is constantly changing position,
makes it absolutely necessary to hold the violin under the chin. To do this in a relaxed
fashion and without tilting the head downwards is extremely difficult; one may lay one's
chin to the left or right of the tailpiece, or, at a pinch, upon it. There is a constant danger, when one descends from the upper reaches of the fingerboard at speed, that the
violin will be torn out from under the chin, or that the even nature of the bowing will
be disrupted by the movement of the instrument.

   The chin rest overcomes all such irritations, not only enabling the violin to be held
in a firm and relaxed manner, but also obviating the need to dampen the vibrations of
resonator or tailpiece by applying pressure through the chin, which heretofore impinged
on the quality and volume of the sound. The act of bowing also benefits, becoming freer
and more regular, since the violin is now held in position directly above the tailpiece at
a greater distance from the face.'

[Textbook excerpt, 1892]

Jürgen W. Braun

The 'Second Aid' phenomenon

or a great way of coming up with new ideas

The history of the second aid begins on the African savannah. There, long ago, a creature with opposable thumbs opened its eyes to gaze upon the world for the very first time. Thanks to this primordial genetic accident, the prehensile hand of our primate brothers and sisters became the precision grip of the subsequent Homo sapiens.

Homo erectus, our not yet terribly aware but slightly more upright ancestor, was no longer able to avoid danger by swinging up into the trees. He was forced to take some other action. Bending down, he grabbed the first stone that came to hand, nowadays named a hand-axe by scientists, and defended himself with it.

Thus the first aid in history was created. A generation later, our by now more intelligent forefathers, drawing on the wealth of experience gained by those who had grabbed before them, grasped something else. They began to distinguish between good-quality hand-axes and poor ones, and also came up with a use for the inferior stones with holes in them: they stuffed branches into the holes, and lo and behold, the second aid was born. At the same time, they discovered the principle of the lever. The branch became a second aid to the 'hand-axe'. The development cycle of artefacts had started. Culture began to emerge from nature.

At the end of the eighties, FSB dedicated *Greifen und Griffe* (Grasping and Grips), the first volume in the FSB series, to the history of the artefact. Authors Otl Aicher and Robert Kuhn relate the history of the artefact and its influence on human thought. In the process, Aicher proves that the history of the development of the artefact has left many traces in the modern German language:

'the relationship between thought and physicality is so close that thought processes are principally expressed in the language of the hands. the soul is apparently not so much anchored in the transcendent as in the hand. because the hand grasps *(greifen)*, so can our minds *(begreifen)*. because the hand touches *(fassen)*, we can comprehend *(erfassen)*. because the hand can put something down *(hinstellen)*, we can describe it *(darstellen)*. because the hand can lay something out *(legen)*, we can explain it *(darlegen)*. and we don't just explain *(darlegen)*, we also consider *(überlegen)*, and either way *(aufeinanderlegen* or *übereinanderlegen)* we pile things up, one on top of the other. we don't just find things out *(feststellen)*, we also put them forward *(aufstellen)*, often as a new proposition. we don't simply understand *(begreifen)* or comprehend *(erfassen)* something, we concern ourselves with it *(befassen)*, we turn it *(wenden)* and twist it *(drehen)*, until finally we come to a conclusion *(Auffassung)* of our own.'

• Key identifiers

So much for the scientifically proven part of the history of artefacts. Looking back, the route taken seems to have been extremely linear – slow, painful, and dogged by trial and error. Gazing into the future, we see this long and painful process still stretching ahead of us. But there's no need to be downcast. And there's certainly no reason for declaring the development of mankind at an end and taking to the treetops again. Indeed, the 'Second Aid' project offers hope.

A brief look inside our department stores will reveal how many good (+) and bad (–) second aids have found their way into our homes:

First in line for some well-deserved praise are the violin-makers. Their chin rests (+) ensure that your hands remain free for the business of playing. Years later, a telephone engineer must have been struck by a similar idea when he invented his plastic receiver support (+), which has since been rendered obsolete by the arrival of the headset. Now I'm sure we've all been entrusted with a well-tied if rather large parcel at some time or another. In that moment, we would no doubt have sent up a thankful prayer for whichever citizen of the earth it was who came up with those handy wire and dowelling handles (+). Rather less beneficial, though serving a similar purpose, are the carrying handles for plastic bags. You can tell just by looking at them that the plastic loops will break, probably sooner rather than later (–). And it's years since we treated our environment with such respect that we were prepared to use up the last inch of pencil with one of those beautiful pencil extenders (+). Continuing in the same vein, plastic pencil grips for the elderly and disabled would seem to make very little sense (–); after all, if people are only able to write with the aid of such a device, how are they ever going to manage to sharpen their pencils in the first place? Of far more use are those casserole dish stands with handles, perfect for serving up hot dishes straight from the microwave (+). On the other hand, Griffboy – meant to enable you to pour milk from a

bag as if from a china jug – overshoots the mark (–). You would hardly be overjoyed if someone decided to package disposable lighters in a way that offers some protection for your fingers (–). And how you can be expected to carry a crate of twenty full beer bottles using a second aid handle is a total mystery. They are so heavy, you have no choice but to use both hands, taking advantage of the moulded openings intended for the purpose (–). By contrast, adapter handles for old-fashioned taps – which disabled people find notoriously difficult to use – are both innovative and functional (+). At first glance, door-handle extensions also seem like a good idea. It's just a shame that the door-handle manufacturers already produce a whole range of handles, short, medium and long, not to mention special models, to suit every requirement (–). On the other hand, key identifiers (+) deserve any amount of praise. They're essential memory prompts. And anyone wanting to try out the round mouse which comes with the newly-purchased iMac will immediately find themselves looking around for an ergonomic second aid to help them out, becoming disciples of design in the process (+).

This brief stroll through an average department store reveals just how innovative we humans are. Second aids which serve a valid purpose are in the majority. Each solution prompts reconsideration. In this sense, the second aid idea represents a great way of coming up with new concepts, refilling the quivers of innovation researchers with bright new arrowheads.

- Carrying handle (+)
- Tetra Pak handle (–)

an idea which we're prepared to try and produce. But most of our products can be found somewhere. The main problem for us is actually locating them. People also write to us. In fact, we've picked up on a couple of things like that. Nevertheless, at the end of the day, you still have to weigh up whether an item addresses a common problem.

The people who contact you – are they mainly inventors or 'modern' housewives?

Scheffold Both. Though we don't get many inventors. Our customers either search through the catalogue and find just what they've been looking for, or they have a problem, don't find an appropriate solution in the catalogue, and therefore write to us with a suggestion. We pick up on it and ask ourselves, 'How many customers will we be doing a favour if we pursue this?' Naturally, we don't want to go to the trouble of having something manufactured, if in the end we're going to sell just three or four of them.

Do you have any designers who are involved in product development?

Forster Not really. Our products are mostly functional items. The manufacturers think up something or other and then market it. Mind you, we do sell a few items where the emphasis is more on decoration than practicality. I suppose there is quite a lot done by designers – you know, furniture, and so on.

Scheffold Our classic products, however, which you refer to as second aids, are all produced to a functional brief.

Are inventors bought out with a one-off payment, or do licences exist which allow them a share of the proceeds?

Forster A bit of both really. We buy out the inventor, or we pay licence fees. Though that's something

of an exception. We discover most products at trade fairs, and companies – manufacturers – also pay us visits. Plus, we also order things from the dozens of brochures and special offers we get sent every day. Of course, we're pretty selective. By the way, I've just found our Schirmboy for pushchairs. *(points to a picture of the 'Umbrella Boy' in the catalogue)*

Scheffold That's a product which is made to our specifications.

And? Is it successful?

Forster It's a very successful product. The Schirmboy has featured in the catalogue now for several years, reappearing every spring and summer. It's proved to be a real winner. Or take this door-mounted clothes hook. It's also made specially for us. It's been in every catalogue since 1972. We didn't buy it from anyone – and we haven't ever seen it anywhere else. It was basically our managing director's idea. He was the one to recognize the problem. So we found a manufacturer to bend the thing into shape, and voila, a new product. Since then, the door clothes hook has appeared in every catalogue and it's almost impossible to imagine life without it.

Which products have turned out to be flops and why?

Scheffold When something's not selling well, Purchasing comes to us and says that the catalogue photo's not good enough. *(laughs)* Sometimes it's simply that things don't work here the way they do in, say, America.

That surely has something to do with standard sizes too. A product that fits a Japanese beverage-can won't necessarily fit a German one, will it?

Forster Precisely. But sometimes we believe so firmly in a product that we try and adapt its design to sell in Europe.

Scheffold I remember one product from the USA. There you can get roof gutters which grow grass and water the garden at the same time. We thought what a great idea and snapped it up immediately, thinking it would work here too. But when the product arrived, we realized it could never work in Germany. In America, roof guttering is completely different and the downpipes don't even reach the ground. Whereas here they go right into it. That's just one example. But there are loads of similar cases. Take the universal door-mounted coat rack. It's a problem because not all doors are the same. The dimensions change as soon as you cross into Belgium or Holland, so you can imagine, if the product comes from America, it quite often doesn't fit at all. In such cases, we either have to adapt the product to suit our market, or drop it from the range altogether.

You offer these racks mainly for doors with a rebated edge. What about the customers who don't realize this?

Scheffold Of course we try to ensure that our products are described as accurately as possible in the text and photos; we show the kind of doors which work and how wide they have to be. But if something doesn't fit, the customer can always return the item.

So you accept returns?

Scheffold As a general rule, nearly all our products may be returned. After all, the customer can't examine the items before purchase, which is why we have a 14-day return policy. Of course, there are a couple of exceptions – things which simply can't be returned once they've been used – such as sanitary articles, videos, CDs, etc.

We were surprised how many things you can buy for the humble door. Why is that, do you think?

Forster A door is perfect for organizing and storing things: you've got coat racks, shelves, video

holders … the list is endless. And then there are things to keep doors open or closed, or secure – childproof. We have just had an offer from a manufacturer producing shoe racks for doors. They hang over the top and can take up to twenty pairs.

Have you already decided to take this product?

Forster We'll probably go for it.

If you do decide to market this product, how large will your trial order be?

Forster Probably something in the region of 1 000 shoe racks.

I assume the rack is pretty large, even when it's packed up.

Forster When it comes to mail order, that's not a problem. Of course, the smaller and lighter the product, the better. But you can't fill 360 pages with small items – there simply aren't enough on the market.

In terms of quantities, what are we looking at?

Forster It varies a lot and largely depends on the price. We've got some products where we sell 20 000 to 30 000 per catalogue, and some where we sell as many as 60 000 to 100 000. We really don't stock any item which sells less than 1 000 per catalogue.

Are there any long-standing customer favourites?

Forster Yes, our thermal cushion. It's been on our books since the very beginning of 'Die moderne Hausfrau'. We've even sold it to the armed forces – to the fighter bomber squadrons. A few years ago, we were continually getting orders from them. The cushion is light, slips into your pocket as easily as a handkerchief, and it's warm and dry to sit on.

We would have thought such an item appealed

Perfect Drawer Organizer

Drawer divider for underwear or socks (Made in Taiwan)

Can be squeezed anything to fit any drawer inside. Trim with scissors to cut any drawer size if necessary. Can be fitted to one side of larger drawers or easily to add more drawer organizers combination for increasing capacity.

[packaging copy]

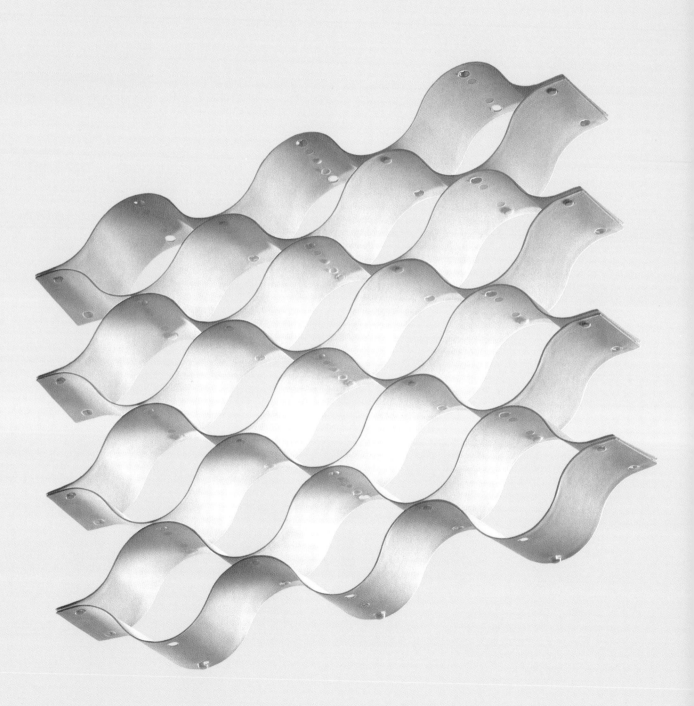

Die moderne Hausfrau

Spring/Summer, Edition 410

Anyone browsing through the catalogue to select one of the 900 or so products will be flabbergasted – firstly, by the inventiveness of the human mind on the subject of housework, and secondly, by the fact that all the items have been found useful. For over thirty years, the longings of German housewives have been satisfied by a mail-order company going by the name of Walz and located in Bad Waldsee, eighty kilometres south of Ulm. 'Die moderne Hausfrau' is published six times a year. The catalogues, which are sent out from Bad Waldsee, offer 'the new and the necessary' by mail order.

[*ZEITmagazin* No. 52, 1997]

Bequemer Autofahren

Autositze fallen zur Lehne hin schräg ab – wer klein ist, kennt dieses Problem. Das spezielle **Autositz-Kissen** gleicht diesen Mangel aus, indem es hinten für mehr Höhe sorgt (besseres Blickfeld), nach vorne jedoch schräg ausläuft, um die Knieposition zum Erreichen der Pedale nicht zu verändern. Mit diesem Kissen sitzen Sie bequemer und aufrechter, erhöhen die Fahrsicherheit, entlasten und schonen Ihre Wirbelsäule und Bandscheiben. Bezug: 100% Polyester.
Nr. 429.660.10 DM **19,95**

vorhe

nachhe

2er-Set *nur* **9,95**

Kennen Sie diesen Sonnenschutzfaktor?

Sonnenschein ist schön und gut, doch im Auto ist Vorsicht geboten. Pralles Sonnenlicht ist jungen und älteren Passagieren schnell zuviel und nimmt allen die Reiselust. Wir empfehlen deshalb den **Sonnenschutz** in origineller Katzen- oder Bärenform. Der ist aus 100 % Polyester, hält das pralle Sonnen-154

licht ab und wird einfach mit Saugnapf a Autofenster befestigt. **Sonnenschutz** – fa haltbar, unverzichtbar! Größe ca. 40 x 4(**Sonnenschutz** mit stabiler Drahtumrand Jetzt im preisgünstigen 2er-Set!
Nr. 504.122.10 „Katze" 2er-Set
Nr. 523.542.10 „Bär" 2er-Set je DM

anorama-Spiegel
send für alle Pkws

Spiegel für mehr Sicherheit!

ch beim Überholen, Fahrspurwechseln
im Einparken bislang eher unsicher
hat, für den ist der **Panorama-Spiegel**
oße Hilfe. Denn bei diesem Spezial-
wird der tote Winkel auf ein Mini-
eduziert. D.h. Sie können den gesam-
um neben Ihrem Fahrzeug mit einem

Blick erfassen, unliebsame Überraschungen
und problematische Situationen werden ver-
hindert! Ja, Sie brauchen auch keinen Einwei-
ser mehr. Der **Panorama-Spiegel** wird einfach
auf den Rückspiegel gesteckt. Passend für alle
PKWs. 26 x 7 cm. Aus Kunststoff.

Nr. 454.281.10   DM **19,95**

Sonnenblenden-Butler

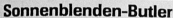

ötigen Parkgroschen,
scheibe oder ein
enn Sie sich heute für
nnenblenden-Butler
iden, brauchen Sie
r im Handschuhfach
len! Einfach Sonnen-
aufklappen, und
aben Sie Ihre
sachen" griffbe-
r Sonnenblen-
ler ist aus
nität gearbeitet
t mit Gummi-

bändern an der Sonnen-
blende. Nutzen Sie die vie-
len Täschchen und Fächer
für mehr Komfort im Auto!
Maße ca. 35 x 17 cm.
Lieferung ohne Inhalt.

Nr. 514.497.10 DM **19,95**

großes Fach für Landkarten,
Parkscheibe, usw.

Fächer für
Ausweise,
Kredit-
karten
usw.

abnehmbare
Täschchen

Notizblock

155

Double Bed Bridger

Our tip: the Double Bed Bridger also works well on hotel beds.

If a great divide carves your marital bed in two, forget marriage guidance and forget the psychiatrist. Your last and only hope is the Double Bed Bridger. Made of inflatable plastic, it fits perfectly between the two mattresses.

   Order the Double Bed Bridger today and discover how two single mattresses can suddenly become wonderfully spacious! Enjoy the absence of cold draughts. Did we mention that it's a cosy spot for the kids? Length 180 cm. The Double Bed Bridger – you know it makes sense!

[Die moderne Hausfrau, catalogue text]

more to the older 'modern' housewife. Do your younger customers buy this product too?

Forster I think the cushion appeals to young and old. It's a very practical thing to have around. Just think of going to football matches.

How long has 'Die moderne Hausfrau' been around?

Forster *(considering)* It all started with the founding of 'Baby Walz'. The company itself produced knitted items and, do you know, I believe they were initially sold from a wheelbarrow. That was in 1954. Then in 1967/68, the company diversified to establish a second sales avenue – 'Die moderne Hausfrau.' A small concern to begin with, it just kept on growing. If you take a look at some of our old catalogues, you'll find, interestingly, that lots of the products are still sold by us today. The colour or shape may have changed. But the problems our customers experienced then were just the same. They too wanted solutions. I wouldn't be surprised if the same problems weren't still around in twenty years' time.

Is it true that the number of products is constantly growing and that the proportion of second aids is also increasing?

Forster Yes, I believe so.

The products shown in the early catalogues seem to have been quite expensive. Nowadays, by contrast, they're more reasonably priced.

Forster In the beginning, we had no direct contact with the manufacturers. We were supplied by importers: middlemen, who relied on their mark-up to earn money. Now we order most things directly from the factory and avoid paying the middlemen.

Who are your customers? Are they really mostly housewives?

Forster Years ago, we were popular with housewives aged between 50 and 70. At the moment, however, the average age of the customer is decreasing. Which means our customer structure has changed. We now have a healthy band of customers aged between 25 and 40. At the same time, the older generation remains loyal.

Scheffold The product range has continued to grow. We're now in the position to provide products for a range of different customers. That's why you'll find youthful, trendy items alongside walking aids for the elderly and disabled.

Are your customers mainly female?

Scheffold Yes, definitely. At least 90 per cent of our customers are women. But we've also got a few house husbands who write to us. They feel discriminated against and are out to 'liberate' themselves. There have already been discussions as to whether we should change the name 'Die moderne Hausfrau'. I personally think it's nice and succinct.

Do you have an in-house name for the products we call 'second aids'?

Scheffold We'd probably say it was a typical 'MH' product. 'MH' is short for 'Die moderne Hausfrau'.

Forster Or a typical mail-order item. Things you can only sell effectively with a catalogue, a nice picture, and good copy; articles which need the medium of the catalogue but also have a certain 'novelty' value.

As product designers, we take these little gadgets seriously. Of course, they have a frivolous side to them – something you play with in your catalogue.

Scheffold Indeed, though of course we have to be careful we don't mislead customers just because we're having so much fun copywriting.

In some circles, your catalogue has already achieved something akin to cult status. Many of the descriptions and pictures could almost be considered satire.

Scheffold That's mail order as it's known in the States. You basically try to demonstrate the problem and its solution as blatantly as possible. In any case, for some products a really clear illustration is essential, otherwise they just wouldn't sell.

Do you all believe that such items are necessary?

Forster Sure. We assume a product works, that our customers need such an item, and that they'll buy it – otherwise, we wouldn't even bother trying.

Scheffold Okay, our existence is dependent on sales. We don't test the products ourselves. But you can bet any product that makes it into the catalogue has our unconditional backing. Of course, the success rate for new products isn't always 100 per cent. But such things are difficult to quantify anyway.

Do you take your customers seriously?

Scheffold Of course. We're not out to mislead or cheat anyone. But it is true that often we only realize what the problem is when we come to the copywriting. I certainly find that sometimes a product lands in Marketing and I have to ask myself, 'What's that for?' Then I take a closer look and think, 'Oh yes, I see.' In other words, it's the product which draws my attention to the problem. And that's exactly how the catalogue works too. The customer reads the copy and thinks, 'My God, that's happened to me before, too,' and orders the product. That's the way impulse buying works.

Forster Some things are used just once and then relegated to the back of a drawer.

Scheffold Of course, the other aspect is the reasonable prices. The resistance against trying something is therefore lower. We also insert some basic psychology into the catalogue texts, phrases such as 'Be the envy of your neighbour' or 'Save yourself the embarrassment'. We're not always quite so direct, but the idea is there.

Forster Or else customers buy articles simply to have something to show off to their friends at the next coffee morning. Afterwards, the item probably won't ever be used again. That's just the way things are these days.

Their worst nightmare

Illustrations: Judith Zaugg Idea: Rolo Bolo, Judith Zaugg

Once upon a time, on a Monday like any other, two Tetra Pak handles were chatting away in the fridge. The older of the two was full of stories about the old days, how she was made in Hong Kong and how, after a long long journey, she finally ended up in Mrs Eversopractical's house. They went on chatting about this and that, saying how happy they were to live with nice Mrs Eversopractical, who always kept them clean and appreciated how well they worked.

But, as the second handle was just beginning to talk about his American home, they heard their mistress coming in with the shopping.

KITCHEN TABLE

NEW DESIGN from ITALY
TETRA PAK HANDLE

The two Tetra Pak handles were very curious. Who would they have to share the fridge with this time – another smelly cheese? That had already happened to them once before – and it was nasty! But maybe they would get new cartons today. However, as Mrs Eversopractical opened the fridge door, the two handles saw something very unusual lying on the kitchen table among the usual purchases.

On the kitchen table lay:
a brand new, totally chic, very arrogant-looking designer Tetra Pak handle from Italy.

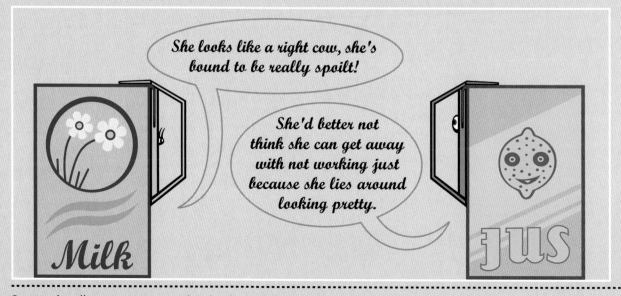

Our two handles were not very taken by the new arrival.

RUBBISH

... and on the same day Mrs Eversopractical brought the two of you home, the poor old milk bag holder was thrown out with the rubbish. I wouldn't be at all surprised if the same thing happened to you.

Indeed, as Granny's old butter dish – a treasured antique – told them of their predecessor's fate, they almost lost their grip.

I am so scared of being thrown away.

Which of us do you think will go first???

Our two second aids were shocked. They had had no idea just how dispensable they were. Now every time Mrs Eversopractical opened the fridge door, they imagined the end had come. They huddled together trembling.

And then something unbelievable happened. Neither of them landed in the rubbish, and the new second aid from Italy made friends with them. She wasn't a cow at all, she was really nice – and she was great at organizing fridge parties.

Journal of a product scout

Three times a year, Hans Jürgen Forster (34) and one of his two colleagues from the purchasing team fly to Asia. Length of stay: between ten days and two and a half weeks. Forster has appointments in various cities, meetings he arranged while still in Bad Waldsee.

His travels take him from Hong Kong to Taiwan, to the Philippines or China. He also trawls for new products for 'Die moderne Hausfrau' in Thailand and Bangkok. Whether using public transport or being driven by chauffeur, Forster can squeeze six appointments into one day, depending on the number of products to be viewed. In the suppliers' showrooms, either alone or in consultation with his colleague, he selects the most promising items. The suppliers are well prepared for his visit. One after the other, they channel him and other purchasers from all over the world past shelves of products. An employee of the manufacturer is in tow to fill out the order lists. Forster himself doesn't speak Chinese. But that isn't necessary, as in Asia business is done in English or German. The countries on his itinerary mainly supply the American and European markets. If necessary, Forster can use an office in Hong Kong for meetings and scheduling appointments. Three hundred Chinese are employed locally under German management to monitor the Asian end of the business. Between appointments, the team also keeps an eye open when visiting the local supermarket. If a product appeals, it is purchased on expenses. Then the manufacturer is tracked down.

When Hans Jürgen Forster arrives back home in Bad Waldsee, he has to wait another two to four weeks for the ordered samples to arrive. His Asian partners ship them on for him – he'd never be able to fit all the samples in his suitcase. On an average trip, he selects 500 to 1 000 items. Some samples arrive bearing an invoice, other suppliers see them as part of customer service and send them gratis.

The catch is viewed in enormous showrooms, in which the 'MH' products of the future are shelved alongside countless former favourites. Between 80 000 and 100 000 products pass through these rooms annually. Here, at the heart of the Walz company, Forster makes the final selection for 'Die moderne Hausfrau'. Most of the new arrivals make it into the catalogue; only occasionally are the team amazed at what they apparently found interesting just a couple of weeks ago in Asia.

The rejected samples are not simply binned, they are donated to the local community as tombola prizes. Which is how a Swabian housewife can

end up owning something potentially unique in the whole of Europe, simply because it didn't make the grade as a mail-order product.

Interestingly, the size of the catalogue illustration which an item receives indicates the degree of faith the company has in the new product, as does the size of the first order: quantities varying between 100 and 5 000 are ordered from the suppliers. Frequently, these trial runs are accompanied by some light-hearted internal betting. Will the 'MH' customer take to the product? Forster's personal tally of products is well above average, which is what makes him such a valuable product scout.

As the first catalogue orders start to roll in, however, he is already on the road again, though not so far this time. He is visiting an inventors' fair in Nuremberg. Forster has already made several discoveries within Germany. The one condition: the idea has to be right and the inventor must be open to product improvements. 'Die moderne Hausfrau' offers the often commercially inexperienced inventor the expertise and the ready market necessary for a successful product launch. Timing is also an essential part of the process.

Bear in mind that it's February right now, and Forster is once more on the lookout for 'products with that special something' – for Christmas!

- Artificial flower factory, Dongan (China)
- Showroom in Taipei
- Showroom in Hong Kong

Christian Donle and Thomas Werle

Second Aids and the law

Second aids are new legal territory.
But one thing's for sure: they exist.

It's not easy to come up with a legal definition. What's certain is that second aids are separate and distinct products, which serve to improve other products, making them more serviceable by overcoming their weaknesses and deficiencies.

A second aid can ruin or enhance the 'parent product'. On the one hand, it may cause damage, on the other, it may bring about a commercial breakthrough. Second aids may serve, damage, offend, enhance, or provide a little extra help. More often than not they simply amaze.

Just like the range of tasks and functions attributed to second aids, their legal status remains unclear. Owing to this lack of clarity, these second aids – from a strictly legal perspective – don't exist. And with that we could simply close this chapter on the 'legal aspects' and elegantly avoid addressing a tricky theme, to the detriment of the reader – though at least we would remain legally untouchable. However, faced with the publishers' editorial might and terminological superiority, that's something the present authors have not even dared to consider.

We will therefore try to approach this topic by examining some of the legal characteristics of second aids, thereafter locating them in the context of the laws pertaining to industrial property

rights and product liability. Second aids are independent products. By nature, however, they are symbiotic, they are parasites of other products, on which they therefore necessarily depend. Without a dripping pot, the drip-catcher is obsolete, the doorstop is lost without a door. Despite this dependence, the second aids and their parent products are rarely drafted by the same designer, let alone produced by the same manufacturer. This is what makes second aids so unusual and also explains their appeal. Moreover, their absolute reliance on the host product relates only to function, and not to any legal relationship. The industrial property rights, for instance, generally enjoyed by the parent product do not automatically extend to the second aid. Any damage engendered by the faulty performance of the host cannot be ascribed to the second aid, and vice versa. In addition, the owner of the rights and those persons liable for the host products and second aids are rarely one and the same.

The lack of legal symmetry between second aids and their parent products causes a number of legal problems for those wishing to design or market a second aid. Their interests are far from uniform. On the one hand, the second aid should make up for the parent product's functional deficiency. On the other, it should be an independent product protected by law from potential pirates and the competition. Finally, the second aid should also profit as much as possible from the market value of the parent product. Since the second aid is obsolete when seen in isolation, it is paramount that any advertisement clearly states for which product the second aid is intended and what extra features it brings.

Second aids seek proximity to the host product. This proximity becomes problematic if the second aid violates the legal rights of the host.

What is allowed? It is the wish of many designers – and the belief of some – that retailers and users may only interfere with their (parent) product design if this has been agreed with the designer in advance. The fact of the matter is rather different. A protective ban is the exception rather than the rule. So it seems as if industrial property rights per se don't often pose an obstacle to the development and sale of second aids.

What kind of protection can the parent product expect? The rights of the parent product generally refer to its design, which may be protected by one or all of the following: copyright, the law on the author's right of personality, the law of registered designs, or competition law.

Does copyright provide any protection? Copyright law offers the most comprehensive protection. Nevertheless, the parent product is cited as an item of copyright in only a handful of cases.

Laws governing the author's right of personality are the legal expression of the ethical and psychological links between an author and his work, in this case a piece of applied art. The author of a work under copyright protection may refuse any changes, revisions, distortions, or similar alterations to his work. He has the legal right to take out an injunction against all persons, even those not commercially active, who engage in such activities. Though an author cannot prevent – and here's the paradox – the destruction of his work, he is entitled to contest every change. Hence the historical decision of the German Supreme Court that though a painter of a risqué fresco has no recourse to justice should his work be completely obscured by a fresh layer of paint, he may forbid the repainting of his bathing nymph's pudenda in the shape of a fig leaf during less permissive times.

Accordingly, from the standpoint of copyright and the author's right of personality, the owner of the rights to a piece of applied art may claim that the aesthetics of his product are compromised by a second aid. Any second aid intending or able to change a piece of applied art – as demonstrated by its advertising or some other aspect, its technical features or dimensions – may be seen as an infringement of copyright. The copyright owner is not obliged to accept any changes to his design.

What about registering the design? Few second aids are likely to be affected by the parent prod-

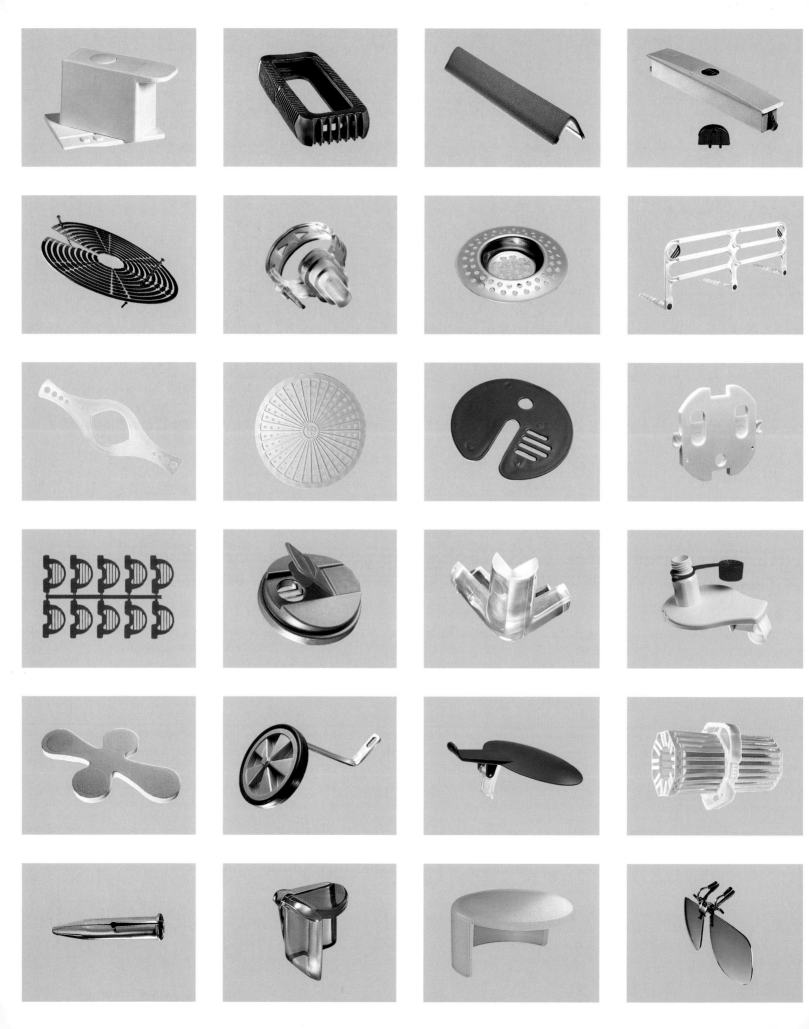

uct's registered design status. 'Features which come under the protection of registered design law are colours and forms, which are designed and intended specifically to appeal to the aesthetic taste of the beholder, … if these represent the work of an individual which goes beyond the … ordinary, beyond the average skill of a designer, without reaching the status of a work of art' is how the German Federal Court of Justice puts it, thereby dispelling all suspicion that it is able to produce elegant definitions worthy of protection. However, one thing at least is apparent: such registration protects 'the design', which at the same time doesn't have to be a work of art (jurists like to talk about 'the degree of artistic expression'). This protection also covers individual sections, elements, or groups of elements. The only condition, according to the definition set down by the German Federal Court of Justice, is that they must be able to be protected. Despite the design proximity to the host product sought by second aids, it is unlikely that protected elements of the host product will be copied. Let's take the iCatch mouse adapter, designed to complement the iMac's iMouse, as an example. It features the same roughened surface and the same colour as the Apple mouse. Its shape, however, is different. Though these similarities of appearance give the impression that the two products do indeed belong together, it is our opinion that this does not violate Apple's registered design. Taken individually or in combination, neither material, surface finish, nor colour can be protected. Without assuming a specific shape, these features – of themselves – do not demand more than 'the average skill of a designer'. The author's right of personality included in copyright law does not apply to registered design law, enabling a violation of this kind to be ruled out.

Does competition law offer any protection?

A conflict between a second aid and its parent product under competition law seems equally unlikely, since competition that is unfair and therefore illegal in the eyes of the law – in the sense of being immoral or deliberately misleading – presupposes a 'competitive relationship'. The second aid, however, is intended to be used in conjunction with the parent product, its purpose being, by definition, to complement rather than replace. Second aids are simply not in competition with their parent products. Nobody would buy the iCatch accessory without first having bought the round iMouse. The second aid exists to promote rather than prevent sales of the parent product. Even though there have been a few isolated cases where, owing to peculiarities of circumstance, the result has been the opposite, the basic assertion, that second aids don't contribute to unfair competition, stands.

What about the law on trademarks? Second aids may be in violation of the integrity interests of a trademark owner. The trademark owner is under no obligation to tolerate commercial changes to his product by a third party which might damage the brand's image. Notorious in recent times have been tune-up centres that specialize in turning luxury cars into the equivalent of boy racer Ford Escorts – for similarly luxurious prices. Though car manufacturers cannot prevent such alterations, they are entitled to forbid such cars from subsequently sporting the brand insignia, such as the Mercedes 'star'. In the case of changes to a product's substance, a manufacturer can demand the removal of the brand logo, since the tangible and actual form of the resultant product is no longer the work of the manufacturer.

Nevertheless, trademark law does not prohibit those marketing second aids from referring to the parent product by its protected product name. Paragraph 23 of the law on trademarks permits the use of a protected product name even when the permission of the trademark owner has not been sought. The use of a protected name is frequently essential to demonstrate the second aid's sphere of application. Thus a manufacturer of spare parts is allowed to name the parent product brand in its advertising. The same is true of the second aid. So that consumers know which

- Oven door lock
- Remote control protector
- Edge guard
- VCR lock
- Pot-plant soil guard
- Doorknob cover
- Sink strainer
- Bed guard rail
- Pan lid retainer
- Sink liner
- Wasp guard
- Safety plug
- Drink protector
- Can topper
- Corner guard
- Can topper
  with drinking spout
- Corner guard
- Stabilizer
- Drinking glass lid
- Scented toilet-rim block
- Pencil tip protector
- Corner guard
- Corner guard
- Clip-on sunglasses

product the item is intended for, the brand name of the parent product may be used. Such use of brand names is not regarded as a breach of trademark law.

Does the patent offer any protection? Even if a host product is protected by patent, second aids are hardly ever likely to be in infringement of it. The protection offered by a patent is limited to the defining features of the invention as recorded by the Patent Office. Only those objects or procedures which use every feature of the protected item, or make use of it, represent a violation of the owner's rights. This is something which, by definition, a second aid doesn't do. It doesn't 'work' like the host; it either complements the parent product, or is used in combination with it. Second aids do not feature the same (technical) characteristics as the host product, and are therefore not affected by its patent.

Second aids are nevertheless at risk: in certain circumstances, they can end up complementing the design of the host product in such a way that the combined result is in violation of a third patent. This happens if the host product does not provide, intentionally or otherwise, a particular and often practical (technical) feature, the rights to which are owned by a third party, and the second aid discovers and rectifies the 'omission'. Intending to serve as complement to the host product, thereby providing it with the missing feature, the second aid lays the foundations for an infringement of the patent rights of the third party. The result is a violation of patent law, which may be contested by the owners of the patent.

What happens if a second aid turns out to be dangerous? Understandably, manufacturers of parent products are only too ready to take legal action – success is practically guaranteed – against second aids if the use of such items suddenly transforms their product into something dangerous. One well-known example from the eighties involved a fairing produced by a manu-

facturer of motorcycle accessories for a particular model. If one of these fairings was fitted, the bike began to lurch from side to side at higher speeds. Many people died or sustained serious injuries as a result. In order to prevent such incidents, parent product manufacturers, importers, retailers, and accessory manufacturers are all obliged to keep an eye on the market and spot any dangerous developments. In addition, products must be recalled, or warnings issued to alert the public to the potential danger. It is therefore essential that the parent product manufacturer have recourse to legal action against the manufacturer of the dangerous second aid, in order to avoid being saddled with the liability – absolutely unwarranted, yet wholly unavoidable.

… or criminal? Second aids are not only to be found in the world of tangible consumer goods, they also occur pretty frequently in the software sector. Computer programs that assist other programs, complementing them or opening additional functions, are especially common. If they do this via pre-arranged interfaces, no copyright objections are usually raised. On the other hand, programs that enable illegal processes (in breach of copyright) are judged according to their intended purpose. A computer program that destroys or circumvents the copy protection of another program, or disables a so-called dongle, without any positive benefit to the program, is treated as breach of copyright or as an offence against the code of fair competition, and as such is prohibited by law.

Can legal protection be exhausted? All intellectual property rights, trademark laws, patent laws, registered design laws, and so on, are subject to exhaustion. Legal protection, trademarks, patents, or the distribution rights of a copyright owner cease to be effective as soon as the product, with the knowledge and approval of the copyright owner, enters circulation. When launching a product, the owner of the rights should be entitled to set the conditions.

He may either receive ongoing licence fees or a buyout sum commensurate with the worth of his intellectual property rights. However, the intellectual property rights of the owner should not enable him thereafter to maintain perpetual control over the product. Generally, as soon as the owner has released his product on to the market, it is considered 'free' of trademark law, patent law, etc. The manufacturer of a product therefore has no recourse to the laws of protection should he wish to prohibit certain uses of the product, or its combined use with a second aid. This is the legal loophole filled by second aids. Although industrial property rights guarantee owners' sole rights of production and distribution, as well as the right to assign a product name (trademark), the product launch effectively annuls any sovereign power the owner has over his product. The property rights are exhausted. The ownership rights of the purchaser now take over. He may do with the product as he sees fit.

Definite exceptions to the principle of exhaustion are different types of negative impact affecting the trademark owner's integrity interests (see negative impact on the parent product above), and the rights of the copyright owner to protect his property against alteration, duplication, or disfigurement.

Can second aids themselves be protected? As far as their own legal protection is concerned, second aids have no special status. Protection against imitation by third parties may be applied for in the form of copyright, or by registering the design or trademark. This affords the second aid some protection against the parent product – of particular value if the manufacturer of the parent product recognizes its shortcomings and decides to integrate into it the second aid's features, or even begins to produce imitation second aids. On the technical side, according to patent law, the second aid is entitled to independent protection rights (by means of patent or design registration). If the parent product itself is protected by technical protection rights, and the second aid has bor-

rowed some of its features, this can also take the form of dependent protection.

Seen from a legal point of view, the design of second aids cuts both ways. Copying the parent product poses legal risks (copyright law, registered design law), yet brings with it legal protection in the form of competitive individuality. Overall, the second aid's function as complement to the parent product is to its legal advantage. It will seldom find itself in breach of the parent product's legal rights, yet at the same time, it is entitled to industrial property protection.

So second aids aren't new at all, legally speaking? It would seem not. What is new is our consciousness of their existence and the creation of a separate category for such items, as they are coaxed out from behind their parent products to bask in the sunlight of a whole world of products.

- Leather seat cushion
- Saddle cushion
- Child's booster seat
- Thermal cushion
- Neck roll
- Wooden bead seat cover
- Chair raisers
- 'Happy back' cushion
- 'TV-Rover' armchair organizer
- Back seat organizer
- Child's car seat
- Woven seat cover
- Bath seat
- 'Spine right' cushion
- WC Clean-Set
- Raised toilet seat
- Non-slip cushion mat
- Chair organizer

Hajo Eickhoff

The thorn and the throne

Helpless helpers

Sitting on chairs is one of mankind's more bizarre postures. Wherever you go, our modern society – which is a sedentary one – will provide you with a chair. Try finding somewhere without a chair or bench. Public and private areas are teeming with places to park your posterior. Whether at home, at work, or on the way somewhere, modern humanity is undeniably into sitting. Unfortunately for us, sitting is neither natural, comfortable, nor good for our legs.

Sitting on chairs has its origin in the throne and was originally a great honour. Structurally, the base of the throne was the block of stone on which humans were sacrificed to the gods. Later, about the time mankind began offering up animals to the gods instead of his own flesh and blood, the stone divided to give us altar and throne. From then on, animals were sacrificed on the altar, and a tribesman, elevated to the status of king, was set upon the throne. The enthroned king, by his very physical immobility, represented a sacrificial victim. A holy being seated on a consecrated throne in a consecrated place. Solitary. Unapproachable and exalted. On the throne, the king learnt to rule his own body: forced by this lack of movement to develop control over his breathing, he acquired the ability to concentrate, to meditate. The posture of enthronement affected body, mind and spirit. By submitting to this discipline, the king became a medium for divine contact. His power transferred to his tribe, while

he became their memory. His mental facility, developed through sitting, made him the creative hub of his society. He remained motionless so that his subjects might move, while looking to him for orientation and meaning.

Sitting on chairs brings no relief. For as throne and enthronement disciplined the king, so chairs and sitting still discipline the populace. Likewise, sitting on chairs restricts movement, forcing the subject to remain still and exercise his grey matter instead. Chairs do not assist the human body; sitting on them does not promote comfort. Sitting on chairs forces the body into an unnatural position and simply means hard work – for your muscles, your intervertebral discs, and your lungs. Second aids attempt to make the tiring act of sitting better and more comfortable by reducing the unnatural aspects, belatedly transforming sitting into a natural activity, which, of course, like all things natural, is in need of improvement. Feet, legs and neck, back, lumbar vertebrae and bottom are relieved, so that sitters can remain thus seated for as long as possible. What second aids promote is the ability to remain in a disciplined posture and the myth that he who sits acquires a royal aspect.

In the eyes of a designer, the chair is a highly desirable object. More energy and creativity are expended on the function and appearance of such furniture than on any other everyday item. This is partially due to the chair's clearly differentiated structure: four legs, a seat and backrest, with or without arms. In addition, there's mobility and image to be considered, the fascination engendered by the direct contact between chair and sitter, the mythological significance of sitting, not to mention the cultural effect of sitting on the inward and outward composure of the subject. As ergonomists began to get involved in the design of chairs towards the middle of the twentieth century, they fostered hopes of being able to develop the perfect chair. But this optimism soon gave way to the widespread opinion that good chairs could only ever help prevent the more serious symptoms of prolonged sitting. Second aids, by contrast, cultivate the illusion that perfect sedentary comfort is obtainable.

Mankind is a creature destined to invent the aid and its second aid. He relies on internal and external organs for assistance. Necessary and trivial. Items which ease his existence. Displaying a tendency to roam beyond the bounds of his immediate influence, he invents and develops tools with which to improve other tools and the objects produced by tools. He creates one aid, and yet another aid to help him produce even more. The world as we know it is the temporary product of a long line of items resulting from other items. A second aid helps the aid to help better. Houses help mankind escape a nomadic existence and climatic dependence, towns liberate him from the natural world. Chairs help him loose himself from his natural condition to find discipline and inner freedom. The human race, once an upright species of 'goers' and 'stayers', has become one of 'sitters'; its point of contact with the world has moved from the sole of the foot to the pad of the posterior. These days, man and the world literally touch base, bottom to chair seat – and for each and every person there now seem to be around two dozen seats.

Chairs are composed of a number of basic aids. The chair legs and chair seat relieve the torso, armrests support arms and hands, while the backrest serves to keep the torso upright. Integral elements of the function and design of the chair, these parts fuse together into a single complex aid. The more designers and ergonomists enquire into the science of sitting, the more aids they build into a chair. Then, when discrepancies arise in practice between the features of a chair and the demands placed upon it, second aids suddenly appear. Various ingenious devices are tried out in an attempt to solve the problem. If one of them causes the problem to disappear, a new second aid is born – an aid of the second degree. These subsequent additions eclipse the original function, or sometimes, more sensibly, the original design.

Second aids express a crisis of function: the misdirected or incomplete development of an object. As opinions concerning posture, its significance, and its effect on the seated subject tend to spring from private conviction and preference rather than actual fact, second aids are big business. Since they correct individual dimensions, they necessarily interfere with other functions, frequently cancelling out important features, or introducing an opposite effect. Second aids rarely focus on design. Solutions which are visually pleasing are therefore few and far between. The chair and the second aid remain at aesthetic odds with each other. It is indeed just this difference between the aesthetic unity of the chair and the visually separate device, which denotes the existence of the second aid, insofar as it remains distinct from the chair's integral features.

The first signs of a personal sitting crisis are the body's natural second aids. Legs are crossed, arms folded, elbows propped up on knees to support head on hands, hands are wedged between thighs and chair seat, or body weight is used to tip the chair forward on to its front legs.

It's about relieving the muscles and supporting the skeleton. Commercial second aids simulate natural second aids: lumbar support provided by the backrest substitutes for the crossing of legs, the backward tilt of the backrest for the holding of the head, and the seat wedge for the chair tilting, which takes the strain off the lumbar vertebrae. Backrest and armrests replace the crossing of arms, seat padding the wedging of hands.

- 'Novelle' toilet seat raiser
- Toilet seat cushion
- Child's toilet seat
- Bath neck cushion
- Bidet/toilet insert
- Gymnastic ball retainer
- Thermal cushion

Seats can be too high or too low. Only a few people are blessed with the standard measurements for which chairs are designed. Swivel office chairs featuring a vertical column on a star base are height-adjustable, whereas four-legged chairs or tubular metal chairs with skids are seldom so. There are many solutions for providing flexibility. DIY enthusiasts insert wooden blocks under chair legs and rails under chair skids, in order to raise the level of the seat for people with unusually long legs. It's also possible to buy such sets ready-made. They are generally blocks of wood or plastic with holes into which the ends of the chair legs are inserted. Second aids of this kind ensure that the seat is positioned at the right height – it is a defining aspect of sitting on a chair that the sitter's bottom should rest at knee height.

Booster seats for children rely on the legs of an existing chair. These foam cushions or rectangular blocks of plastic, with or without backrests and armrests, can be positioned on chair seats. The child sits on the booster, which is ten to twenty centimetres high, with his feet resting on the chair seat. There is even a 'table seat' for the very young, so that children can participate in family mealtimes from an early age. While the table seat appears to be a chair in its own right, it is really only a complex second aid for the chair leg: a steel frame cradles a seat with fabric panels at the sides and back for extra safety, and a screw clamp arrangement is used to fasten the whole thing to the table. A safety harness prevents the child from standing up. The table seat classically illustrates the social expectations of a sedentary society, which has inserted an intermediate stage into the natural progression from lying to crawling to walking – a 'sitting stage' between lying and crawling.

The main feature of all chairs, sofas and benches is the seat: mankind's main point of contact with a material base. The seat may be horizontal, angled up or down, made of wood or plastic, or upholstered. The upholstery, in any number of fabric covers, can be hard or soft, flat or rounded, simple or multilayered. Modern office chairs offer the widest variety of seat types: designed like a saddle, divided symmetrically, or tailored to match the shape of the human bottom. Cushions account for a large number of the second aids available for chair seats: as decoration, extra padding, or repair element. Padding is supposed to prevent poor circulation caused by long periods spent sitting, while expensive extra seat cushions add value to the chair. Wedge-shaped cushions serve a particular function. Cushions themselves may also receive a little help, in the form of protective covers, or cushion mats to prevent them slipping off angled seats.

Even the sophisticated high-tech office chair, developed in accordance with ergonomic principles, is not necessarily safe from second aids. Second aids which concentrate on posture, extolling their virtues with naive assurance, prey on common misconceptions, often to the detriment of existing functions; this is amply demonstrated by a standard wedge cushion with the pompous medical name 'orthopaedic "spine right" cushion'. The specially shaped seat of the office chair chosen to display the effect of the wedge cushion is designed to complement the chair's backrest, helping to push its bulging form against the lumbar region and thereby prevent the sitter from getting a round back. In fact, the seat and backrest cannot guarantee this result, since the upright posture promised by the manufacturers can only be maintained by a chair – and then for a limited period – if the sitter also remains conscious of it and actively uses it against overtaxed and fatigued muscles. The addition of a wedge cushion puts the sitter in a position that's impossible to maintain. It simulates sitting on a chair that is tipped forward, which in theory should be beneficial; however, it also puts integral features of the office chair out of action, thereby making the situation worse than it was before. The ergonomic shape of the chair becomes useless and the support offered is lost: the depth of the seat is lessened, since the lumbar support offered by the backrest no longer pushes against the lower

back, but instead against the pelvis, which now protrudes further; moreover, by raising the torso, the backrest of the chair and the spine of the sitter are no longer parallel to each other, making the backrest unusable. In practice, this means either that the wedge is soon discarded, or that muscles and vertebrae are damaged by continued use. A wedge cushion can only be used effectively on the flat seat of a chair with an unshaped or height-adjustable back. The fact remains, however, that even when sitting on such a chair, where the seat is tilted forward at an angle, correct posture can only be guaranteed by a conscious effort on the part of the sitter.

The mythological significance of a chair is most clearly expressed by its backrest. The king was not wont to lean against it. The back of the throne symbolized protection, vocation, anointing: during enthronement ceremonies in Ancient Egypt, the high priest stood behind the pharaoh elect. He laid his arms on the shoulders of the heir to the throne and anointed him as pharaoh. The high priest embodied Horus, the hawk-like god, whom the pharaoh became during his enthronement. The back of the throne stood for Horus, for protection, and for the moment of anointing. Today, the height of the backrest distinguishes the managing director's chair from all others. The chairs in a company are all subordinate to the quality and look of the managing director's chair. The backrest which towers highest above the head of the sitter remains the prerogative of the boss. A few second aids designed especially for chair backs aim to add visual status to ordinary chairs. Such compensation is either presented as an obvious increase in status and value, or is camouflaged under the pretence of comfort (e.g. the 'happy back' cushion).

Armrests are increasingly used as arm supports by those who work at computers; this is reflected in a variety of possible adjustments. Since armrests vary enormously in shape, their second aids must be adjustable – things are stretched over the rests or wrapped around them, giving

the impression that the chair is injured and has had to be bandaged.

Car seats are subject to a whole range of demands. Cars are in effect mobile chairs. High-tech armchairs. Seats without legs, variously adjustable, and designed to offer the greatest degree of support when cornering and braking. As well as seat belts designed especially for children and pregnant women, an entire range of second aids exists to take happy advantage of the absolute inertia of the car driver and passengers: seat boosters, back cushions, leather seat cushions, back seat organizers, and child seats for the back seat. Back seat organizers provide the modern traveller with all the necessary travel essentials. Hung from the backrest by means of a metal hook or fastened to the headrest using press studs, such organizers help keep cars tidy, while providing quick and easy access to snacks, maps, toys, and magazines. Taxi drivers, travelling salesmen, and the like often make use of a beaded seat cover to combat the effects of hours spent sitting. They happily go without the comfort of a smooth upholstered seat, since the massage effect and the improved air circulation brought about by the wooden beads, which are able to move separately, stimulates blood circulation and helps to keep the back muscles flexible.

The longer a person sits, the more dependent he becomes on sitting. The strain of standing up grows. That's why second aids aim to bring everything needed for a period of work or an evening of television within reach of the sitter. The 'TV-Rover' armchair organizer, a fabric receptacle which hangs over the armrest like a back seat organizer, offers compartments for listings, magazines, glasses, the remote control, and a host of other things. The portable chair organizer is intended for the same purpose when away from home.

If someone is no longer able to get up from a chair because of age or illness, there are devices which can help. The lift, a separate mechanism that can be attached to any chair, brings the sitter to a standing position. Exerting pressure on the armrests or leaning forward sets off the lifting

- Chair seat cushion
- Folding seat cushion
- Wedge cushion

- Furniture raisers

spring mechanism. This second aid dispels the anxiety of being stuck in a chair, unable to communicate with the outside world. Other second aids ease the action of sitting down. Additional second aids for weak or disabled individuals include bath seats, raised toilet seats, toilet seat cushions, orthopaedically designed seats, folding shower seats and inflatable cushions. From childhood onwards, mankind grows into his chair, until he and the chair finally become one. The range of tasks assigned to second aids by the elderly and infirm and on which they depend should not be underestimated.

Even unconventional perches such as the gymnastic-ball seat don't get away without a couple of second aids. Dish-shaped retainers, which keep the ball in place, are common. They are meant to check the force which pushes the ball forward under the weight of the sitter, a force that is otherwise absorbed by the ankle joints. Since the relief brought about by such retainers is marginal, designers have come up with a tubular frame in which to place the ball. The ball becomes a chair, thereby losing much of its dynamic, flexible character.

Second aids can also be invisible. Just consider the range of physical exercises designed for those with a sedentary lifestyle. These concentrate on releasing pent-up energy, caused by a reduction in movement, in a variety of situations and using a range of objects: at the table, in the car, in a chair, using machinery, using beer crates. At training courses in sitting, movement programmes are practised under supervision. Imaginary second aids target the body and the consequences of sedentary inertia directly. These days, some companies are encouraging employees to think on their feet, literally, and make use of 'thought corridors' set up especially for the purpose. To be able to sit, mankind needs to keep on moving.

We can assess these second aids using the following criteria: their interpretation of the act of sitting and their effectiveness. One category which emerges is the pseudo second aid. It only serves to mislead the consumer: it either doesn't help at all, or causes actual damage by cancelling out the existing functions of a particular chair. At best, it addresses elements which simply relate to the mythology of sitting – to authority and anointing. Such second aids are nonsensical and merely reinforce common misconceptions. They are ideological rubbish.

The other category of second aid is the intermediary, a small step in the direction of the modern chair, the product of chair-related technological progress. Though aesthetically out of place, these afterthoughts correct functional flaws, and are generally destined to be incorporated into later models, thereby achieving the status of integral aid. The best of the second aids are the body's own strength and the many alternatives to the chair – lecterns, reclining chairs, oriental floor cushions, kneeling in the diamond position, or standing chairs. Since they promote movement by stimulating frequent changes in posture and breaks from sitting, they quite simply prevent sitting from becoming a thorn in your flesh.

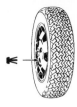

Wheel marker

For steel and alloy rims – fits all popular makes

Mark your wheels when changing them. Mark wheels without any problems when changing
between winter and summer tyres – avoid unnecessary wheel balancing and alignment.
Simply put the wheel marker through a hole in the rim (the wheel-nut hole) and the wheels are
distinctively marked. Wheels can be stacked and washed – markers cannot smudge or fall out.
Can be used over and over again – in summer and winter.

[aroso, packaging copy]

saying they want to do this and that? Or do they simply go ahead, having looked at the new model and decided what can be tinkered with?

sacco Well, I would say the latter. It's actually become quite difficult to discuss car design, especially changes in visual appearance, with a company that's relinquished most of its stock to Daimler-Chrysler.

We were under the impression that these guys were the goodies (pointing to the AMG catalogue) and these the baddies (pointing to the latest car accessory catalogue).

sacco *(laughs)* Sorry, but whose catalogue is that?

Jörg Tuning. We bought it from a news-stand in Stuttgart.

sacco Jörg Tuning! Well, okay, you're right, they are the baddies. *(laughs)*

We thought the conversation might go something like this: 'Let's see, after two or three months of the A-Class ... is there something we could remove to give the car a facelift? We're not just talking about a functional alteration, we're thinking of changing the shape of the headlights.'

sacco *(looking at a headlight accessory in the catalogue)* That was a popular attachment for the W 123, a model produced from the mid-seventies to the mid-eighties. Because it gave the headlights a more diagonal look, it made you think you were looking at a newer model, particularly from a distance. That's all it was designed for.

Just like this thing here (pointing to another catalogue illustration). It imitates the S-Class and calls itself the 'S-Look' grille.

sacco Never! Really? They're horrible ... But then I have to admit, I've never looked at such a catalogue before. What would be the point? You can't

prevent it. Any legal leverage is limited to registered trademark protection. The brand's independent status is protected in so far as the altered products in question are no longer allowed to carry the brand insignia. For instance, Brabus customizations may not display the star or the name of Mercedes-Benz. Everyone knows these cars were originally Mercs, but now they bear the tuner's name instead of the star.

So that's obviously where the Mercedes ends.

sacco Yes, because then you're getting into warranty issues which have nothing to do with the manufacturer. If Brabus does this or that to the car, it's to be expected that it will give up the ghost sooner rather than later. For this reason, the company ceases to guarantee the vehicle by stating that it's no longer a Mercedes.

But isn't the particular style also something which comes under warranty?

sacco The monetary aspect of any warranty claim is our main concern. Of course, in really tasteless cases, we can always insist on the star being removed!

The merits of each individual case are decided separately?

sacco Of course! Which is why our legal department always has its work cut out at car shows. But that's normal.

But then you've also got people who decide to decorate their Citroën 2CVs with a Mercedes grille and star.

sacco Well, there's not much you can do about that. I find that less problematic. Once, I even saw a small car which had been fitted with a Rolls-Royce radiator grille. You see that kind of thing and you smile. There's nothing wrong with a bit of fun! And besides, we're not likely to get any warranty

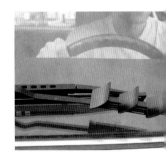

▪ Contact pressure amplifier

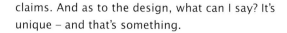

claims. And as to the design, what can I say? It's unique – and that's something.

Do you ever lose your sense of humour when driving on the motorway? Constantly being confronted with your designs, even when they're practically unrecognizable. Last summer, black net sunshades in the shape of a cat's head were all the rage, attached with suction cups to the car windows. Is that something which irritates the professional car designer? Aren't you tempted to point out that if you've already got tinted windows such items are superfluous? Or do you just accept it?

Sacco Naturally. All our designs are registered years before a new model is brought out, the main purpose being to prevent anyone from copying components and trying to pass them off as original Mercedes parts. But of course people will occasionally plagiarize one of your ideas.

So that means that, say, the rear right-hand wing of a Mercedes is a registered design?

Sacco Yes, yes. The same goes for the rear apron, the lights, wheels, and various other parts – in fact, usually those that need replacing most often. The radiator grille also comes under design protection.

A question about 'facelifts': when a model bought just a couple of years ago suddenly looks old because of recent design changes – surely in this case, such accessories give owners the chance to pep up their cars?

Sacco Okay. Of course, there are people who'll buy some self-adhesive gimmick for a couple of Euro, but who's to say it won't fall off! To really keep up with the latest facelift, you'd also have to buy the bonnet and the radiator grille. Then you'd at least look up to date. However, while we're on the subject, I'd like to point out that in the ten years Mercedes produced the 190, there was only ever one facelift – during the sixth year. And I'm sure, bearing in mind how long it stayed in production, that

those who bought one of the first 190s and later decided to buy a second one had nothing against the latter's slightly more modern appearance. The facelift certainly wouldn't have disadvantaged those owners who still had the 'older' version. Though I can say that a facelift – an invisible one – actually takes place every year. Once a year, every car manufacturer replaces a few parts in the whole equation. It's true. Parts which maybe haven't shown themselves to be particularly reliable. I'm talking mainly about alterations under the bonnet, things you generally wouldn't notice anyway.

That's something else we wanted to ask you about. Maybe, after hours of driving time, you feel something's missing and begin to …

Sacco … in this catalogue, you'll find that maybe 0.01 per cent of the products fall into that category – I'm prepared to say so, even though I haven't studied it closely … (laughs)

But what about cup holders?

Sacco There was a time several years ago when we didn't include cup holders; they simply weren't part of our concept. Now all Mercedes cars have them. Because it was released in 1989, the SL only got one later. There really isn't a single Mercedes model on the market that doesn't have one or two cup holders. That's why you're only likely to find such accessories designed for older Mercedes models.

For decades, people have been coming up with solutions for drinks in the car. They've usually been plastic devices which you insert between windowpane and door panel. Were they what prompted you as a designer, or the company of Mercedes, to consider a standard solution seriously?

Sacco Of course we were prompted! It got to the point where everybody had one of these holders. But once we'd effectively penetrated the American market, it became essential for Mercedes. We soon

• Car door armrest

learnt from our customers over there that a car without a cup holder would be hard to sell. Americans won't buy a plastic accessory and stick it down the side of the door panel, they just won't buy the car if it doesn't have a cup holder. They'd rather buy a different make instead.

It's incredible that such a detail should be the deciding factor in whether or not to purchase a car.

Sacco I think so, too. But it's also revealing how slow our marketing people were to pick up on it. They really thought it ridiculous that someone interested in buying such a quality car could possibly place so much importance on a cup holder.

Do you think this hook could be next in line? (points to a shopping bag holder)

Sacco That? No, that's far too dangerous! Its position would be extremely dangerous for anyone sitting in the front, even if they were wearing a seat belt.

And what about the seat belt extender for kids?

Sacco It's simply unnecessary. Younger children should sit in proper car seats and older children don't need it. That's been proven. The manufacturers are basically out to make money.

To return to the previous topic for a moment, to what extent do such makeshift solutions influence the design process? For instance, the cup holder. Did the design idea arise out of the existence of the accessory, or was it produced in direct response to market demand? Were the customers saying they needed such a thing?

Sacco If we consider the global car market, I really can't say whether the accessory came first, or whether – and if so, it could only have been in the States – cars were conceived, designed, and built with such a fitting, and this makeshift solution arose as a copy. I honestly don't know. But at Mercedes, we didn't copy these accessories.

For years, American and Japanese cars have featured cup holders as integral interior elements. As far as 'copying' is concerned, almost every interior requires the creation of a new and unique solution, kinetically tailored to its possible installation. The range of movements envisaged by our engineers for these holders has frequently amazed me.

Would you say, therefore, that you have rarely, if ever, developed a design using one of these makeshift solutions as your starting point? What about those extra brake lights which you mount on the back ledge behind the rear windscreen? They were the height of fashion during the eighties. Everyone had these extra lights. Now there are lots of cars on the road which feature such brake lights as standard.

Sacco Oh yes, I even know a couple of people who had them. They weren't interested in the safety aspect, they just thought they looked good. The whole trend arose out of a discussion which was set in motion at the beginning of the seventies with the development of ESVs (Experimental Safety Vehicles). These were cars in which the strapped-in occupants could theoretically survive a head-on collision with a wall at 80 kph without air bags. They also featured a number of other extreme safety precautions that the accessory manufacturers were swift to pick up on. The third brake light you just referred to – a further development of these tests at the beginning of the seventies – is doubtless a sensible idea. By the way, it also comes from the States. It definitely wasn't invented by the accessory industry; it was copied from these safety vehicles and then developed.

Is it possible that these accessories simply provide the owners of older cars with the chance to buy features that are standard in newer models?

Sacco Of course, that's one possibility. I really don't want to suggest that all of these accessories have nothing to offer. But the question remains

- Universal steering wheel knob
- Contact pressure amplifier
- Cup holder
- Universal hands-free holder for mobile phone
- 'Cat' sunshade
- Anti-static strip
- Car door armrest
- Towing mirror
- 'Aerodynamic' wiper arm boot
- Shopping bag holder

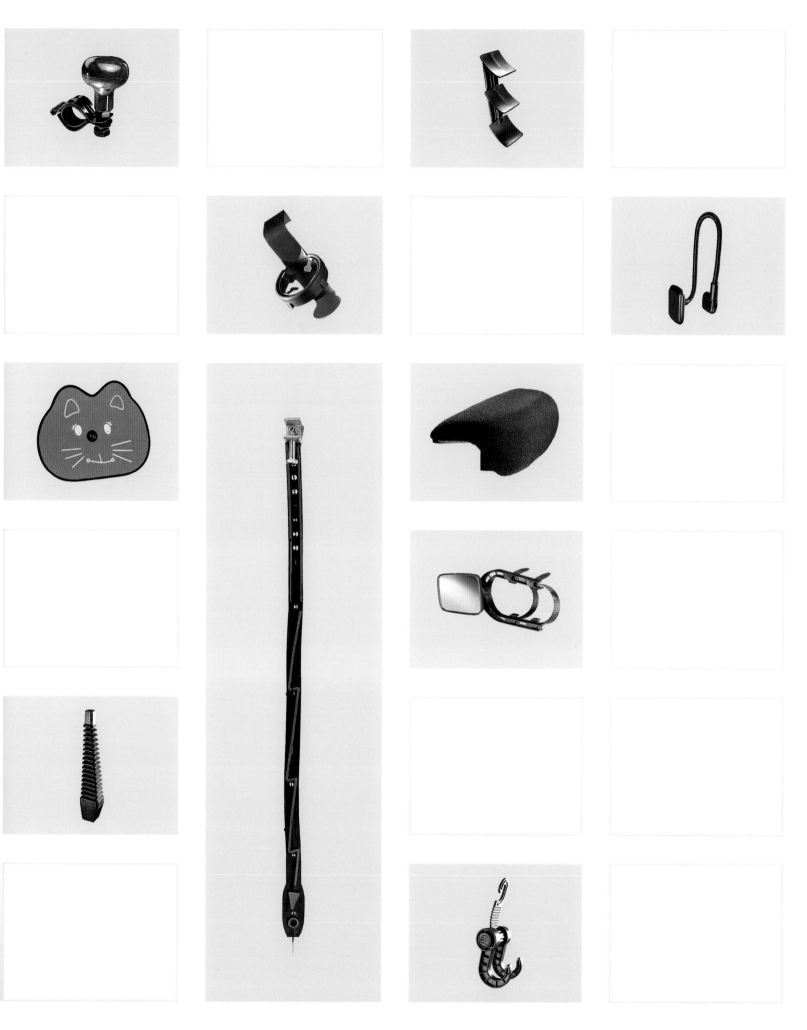

whether the item compromises the safety of the car. *(points to the hook again)* The manufacturer who made this hook will have produced tens of thousands of them.

Okay, let's pretend I'm the car designer. I may think the shape of the product is dangerous, but I realize it fulfils a need. So I come up with something comparable, in the form of a professionally designed standard fitting.

Sacco Yes, but you couldn't position it here. Even if there was a demand from customers wanting somewhere to hang a bag, you couldn't put the hook here. You'd have to sink it into the door panel. But I must say that in my forty years as a designer, I have no knowledge of such a demand. On the other hand, I am well acquainted with the need for some kind of a hook next to the passenger seat, some kind of ledge for women's handbags. I personally don't know what to do with my bag if I'm driving somewhere *(pointing to his own wrist-bag)*. I just lay it next to me on the front seat. A hook would only be practical if you could position it within reach, and then it would be in the way for both driver and passenger. It would constantly be banging against your knees. There is no real place for handbags, which generally belong to women, in cars. I consider that a serious problem.

But even so, you've never submitted a design that might solve it?

Sacco Oh yes, I have. I've come up with countless proposals! But whichever way you look at it, each solution just ends up getting in the way. It's sad, but unfortunately that's the way it is.

You say there are customers who request solutions. Does Mercedes-Benz have a department which deals with such requests? And do these occasionally land on the designer's desk?

Sacco Yes, and not only at Mercedes. The same goes for every car manufacturer. I really don't want to speak solely on behalf of Mercedes. I've quoted a few examples from Mercedes because I know the company well. However, I'm not here to talk to you as a Mercedes spokesman. Firstly, because I'm retired, and secondly, because it makes no sense. The majority of car manufacturers do exactly the same anyway.

And it's your opinion that, regardless of the manufacturer, customer requests really do end up on the designer's desk at some point or other?

Sacco Yes, yes, of course they end up on the designer's desk. Let's take the old chestnut of where to put the handbag. I first encountered this request about thirty years ago. There was no solution then either. We tried out a soft hook (anything else and you'd have been banging your kneecaps on it all the time). Then came a hook which was recessed in the gap between the front seats, but that was a bit awkward. And besides, nowadays that space is generally occupied by a mobile phone holder. More recently, we developed the combined mobile and handbag holder. That's something you could add a hook to. You wouldn't believe some of the weird and wonderful things we've tried out.

And what's your line on the best place for a mobile?

Sacco Mercedes produces a car telephone. A hands-free arrangement. That's absolutely essential, since mobiles in cars can be extremely unsafe. But it's also unsafe to use your mobile in hands-free mode, because you've still got to dial. Telephones in cars are only likely to become safer with the introduction of voice controls. The race is on at the moment to produce such a product, the hope being that it'll be the norm in a few years' time. Of course, anyone who owns a mobile rather than a car telephone is first of all going to look for a place to put it. I've got out of the habit of using my mobile while driving. I keep it in my bag and if I have to telephone, I pull over.

We're impressed!

Sacco I'm not just trying to set an example. I got into real trouble once ... I've learnt my lesson ...

And here's another page of this car accessory catalogue.

Sacco Hmm, wheels. *(laughs)*

We've noticed a tendency among designers to re-move the hubcaps from their wheels and drive around displaying the black rims.

Sacco That's fine with such wheels, with proper pressed wheels. Designers are known to be purists. I also drove for a while without hubcaps. Of course, the best solution would be a wheel that's so nice to look at you don't need hubcaps. That would be ideal, and that's something we've attempted several times. In fact, we do produce a car which has beautiful wheels as standard. They're aluminium – not cast, but pressed. That's the CLK sports version. But even the basic A-Class has aluminium wheels. We worked very hard at this particular feature. It's not easy to combine functional requirements with designer good looks. In this case, we wanted to produce simple wheels, as an optional extra. For all those individualists out there.

On the subject of individualization, who was the A-Class aimed at? Did you have a particular type of customer in mind, for whom it would represent the perfect car?

Sacco Now you're talking about something much broader than the concept of wheel design. You're touching on the general design of a car – of which the wheel is only a small part.

Indeed. But for each car, there is a basic model, and there are the optional extras, which are sure-ly an expression of the desire to customize. So the question remains whether as a designer, you have

a type of person in mind when designing a partic-ular car. Do you ask yourself, for example, who are these people who go for the A-Class, yet at the same time still want such horribly thick hubcaps? Or, to put it another way: by offering a range of different cars, are you prescribing vehicles to fit certain types of customers?

Sacco I beg your pardon, I don't think so! There are more wheel types for the SL than for the A-Class, although you would expect the SL – as you so rightly say – to attract a certain type. You would think that since the customer has already decided on a sports car, he will therefore want sporty wheels. But that's simply not the case! You have a much larger choice of wheels and tyres with the SL than you do with the A-Class. And that's not something imposed by the car manufacturer, it's a response to demand.

Maybe that's because drivers of sports cars tend to be more individualistic than other drivers.

Sacco Okay. That's a possible explanation, even a likely one. But I believe the desire to individualize is so deeply ingrained in all of us, that there are very few people who don't succumb to it.

Judging by your tone, I'd say you view that rather negatively.

Sacco No, it's just something I've noticed.

In theory, therefore, you have to come up with designs that allow for as much subsequent indivi-dualization as possible.

Sacco Actually, no. That's never been our expressed intention.

But maybe it would be worth thinking about.

Sacco Er ... mmm ... no, no, no. Then you'd end up producing car shells – for customers to decorate like Christmas trees. No, no, no! On the contrary,

▪ 'Bear' sunshade

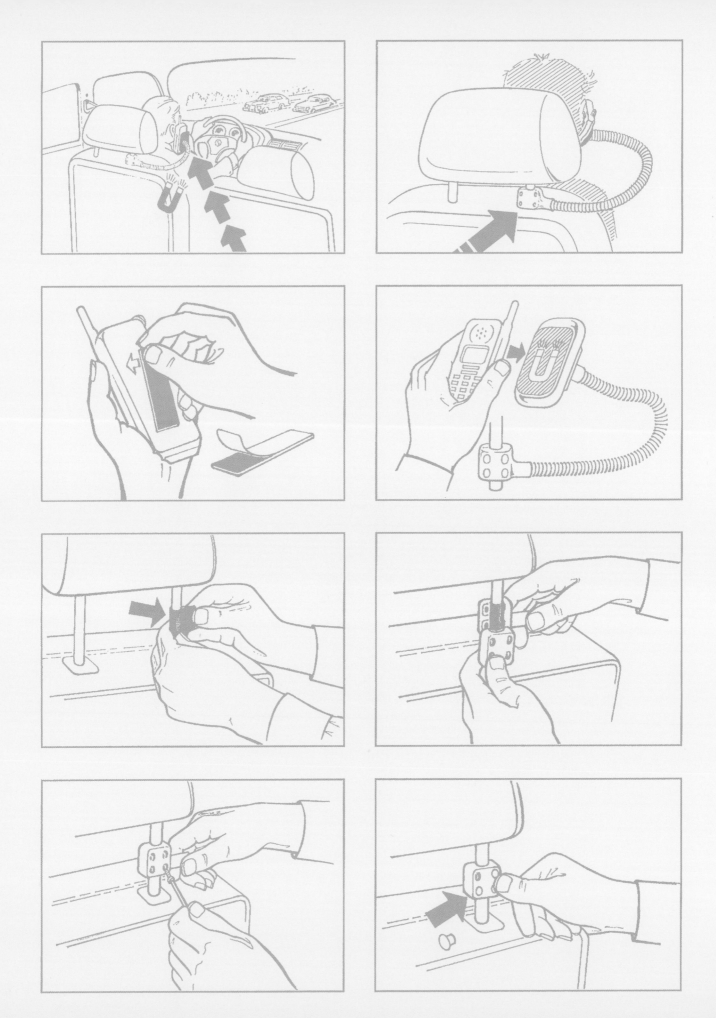

we frequently try to cut down on the number of extras. As far as wheels are concerned, there's not a lot you can do, because …

… it's so easy to take them off and replace them with new ones?

Sacco Exactly!

Is each Mercedes a reflection of your personal taste?

Sacco No, not really. If I were to design a car for myself, then of course it would be. But when it's a product conceived as a result of teamwork, after much discussion and analysis, it no longer reflects my taste but the collective taste of the team. Of course, it can happen that a team develops tunnel vision after a while and ends up thinking only in terms of Mercedes. Though the make-up of the team changes so often that this is hardly possible.

Do you drive the basic version of your car – which is one of your own designs, I believe? Or have you made a couple of changes?

Sacco I didn't need to change anything. I could give free rein to my creativity in choosing the upholstery and the colour. Which is why I went for a black car, with black upholstery and black wood. If I'd wanted, I could have chosen very unusual materials from the 'Designo' range – awful word, don't you think? The only thing in my car which I really didn't want is the burlwood dash. It wasn't my choice and I would have chosen another finish, but it was too late, so I just have to put up with it.

What do you mean 'too late'?

Sacco When I ordered the car, I spontaneously went for something quite different. Nevertheless, they did their best to get me the car I finally decided on. But, unfortunately, it was too late to accommodate this extra. Once I got the car I could have had it swapped, but I'm prepared to live with it.

We'd never have thought that a Mercedes-Benz designer would be prepared to accept even the tiniest detail in his car which wasn't a reflection of his own taste. That says a lot for your self-control.

Sacco Sure. But I think it also has something to do with age. As you get older, you become more tolerant. I think you develop a more practical outlook. When I'm driving, I simply don't look at the wood. It's far more important to me that the car drives as I want it to. It's only really if I'm sitting at traffic lights that I …

But otherwise the car is unchanged – just as Mercedes delivered it?

Sacco It does have a few functional extras, such as air conditioning.

You mentioned 'Designo'.

Sacco Yes, 'Designo' is something very special. However, you have to decide several months in advance what you want to have done; in advance, that is, of the car being completed. Because production is computer-controlled, there comes a point after which you can't make any more changes to a standard car. The more popular the car, the fewer changes are possible.

Which is why such catalogues as these exist.

Sacco Indeed. In case someone discovers, having purchased a car, that he'd prefer this or that feature a little different. If the parts need mounting, of course you can drive along to a garage and get a few things replaced. It just costs more money, that's all.

What about this sunblind here? (points to the product)

Sacco You can buy such blinds as standard. The blind is set into a recess in the rear shelf. This blind is a makeshift solution. A frame that you

▪ Universal hands-free holder for mobile phone

can attach if you've forgotten to buy or order a blind with your car.

Would that be an example of something you wouldn't be able to fit post-production?

_{Sacco} No, there would be no problem fitting it. But since it's an organic solution, it would cost a little bit more. You'd have to swap the rear shelf for a new one and mount the lower section underneath. This here is a quicker alternative for someone who discovers he forgot to order one at the right time. I personally have nothing against such things.

I've just glanced at my watch and I see that our planned five-minute chat about second aids has become an interview of one and a half hours. I hope you haven't found it too boring.

_{Sacco} Quite the opposite. Otherwise I would have made my excuses already. After all, I too came here to be entertained.

  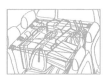 

- Shopping bag holder
- Wooden bead seat cover

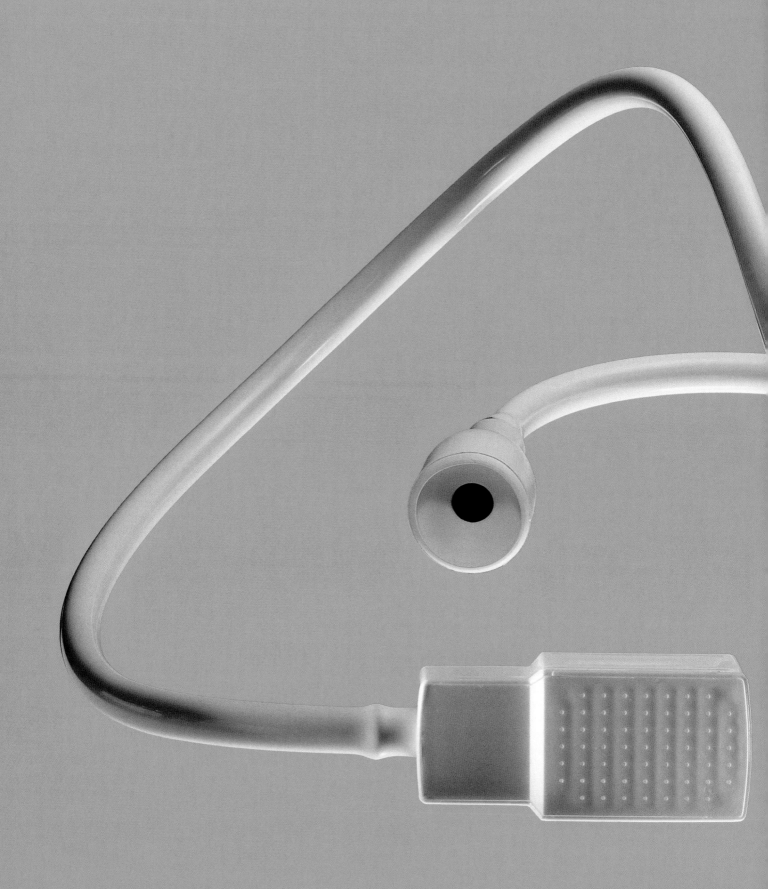

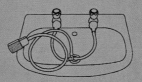

Duet Shampoo Spray

At the forefront of shower technology (Made in Britain)

Easy to fit. Just wet the rubber connectors before fixing. Made from strong PVC, rubber and ABS plastic. This appliance should not be connected to taps which deliver domestic hot water at a higher temperature than 70° centigrade. Higher temperatures may damage the appliance and scalding could occur. (66° C is the maximum temperature recommended to avoid excessive scaling of pipes and is usually the maximum temperature set on installation of immersion heaters).

The push-on connectors must not be permanently fixed to the taps with clips or other retaining devices.

[Aqualona, packaging copy]

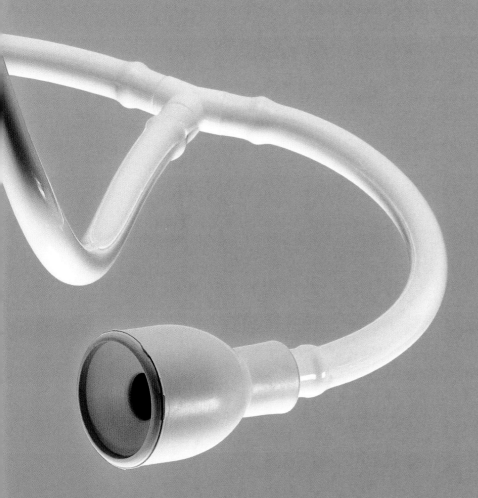

Milk bag holder

For milk in bags

Practical! Hygienic! Eco-friendly!

[packaging copy]

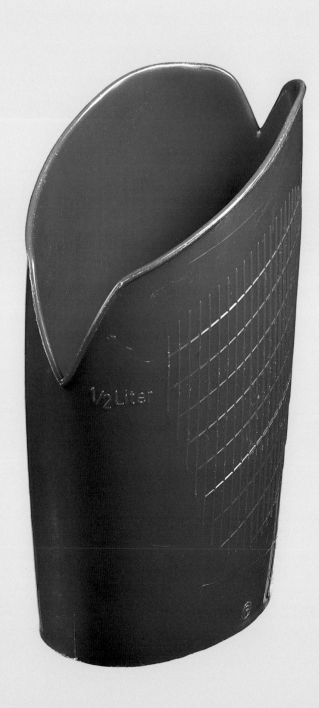

1/2 Liter

Fish-bone plate

Simply clip on to the edge of your plate

A tasteful solution for fish bones and other table waste!

Bernhard Wördehoff

The book cover Embroidered by generations

Occasionally one still comes across a handmade book cover. For decades, it was one of the prime products of female handicrafts. The book cover was an expression of a bourgeois era of thriftiness, which sought to conserve and protect everyday objects. The spectrum of safeguards ranged from protective coverings for furniture and lamps in the front parlour (the 'salon' of the haute bourgeoisie) to rubber overshoes for protecting footwear when it rained.

In the making of book covers, certainly a very individual task, various materials were used, such as cardboard, linen, and even fine leather. However, the most popular material was the finely woven starched canvas that forms the basis of cross-stitching.

Cross-stitching gave the book cover the personal touch required of a handmade present. The motifs were practical and sensible, brightly coloured flowers perhaps, or simply the monogram of the person giving or receiving the present. When using canvas, the book cover was lined with a soft fabric, so that the binding of the volume being covered would not be damaged by the reverse side of the cross-stitching. By providing ties, pockets and elastic bands the needleworker tried to ensure that the binding of the book could be fastened to the cover. Usually in vain, however, as the book often rattled around disastrously inside the cover or even fell out of it, because book and cover rarely fitted each other perfectly. Often the book cover proved to be a white elephant, something to be tolerated – like the fretwork key holder.

In the end, is it really the perception that the book cover has a limited use that killed it off, after decades of tenacious survival? Is it part of the forgotten era of crochet bags and embroidery frames, another victim of the evolution of home crafting into the do-it-yourself movement? Perhaps. But we may rather assume that the book (like the lamp) is no longer seen as an article that warrants special protection. An absurd idea: a book cover to protect a paperback. But even the modern hardback can scarcely be imagined in conjunction with a book cover, an endearing old antique for all its faults. Books have become cheap goods (to speak only of their prices). Gone are the days when the publishing business operated on the costing principle attributed to the publisher Kaspar Witsch: a book can cost as much as a shoe (strictly, as half a pair of shoes). Since then, the prices of shoes have put on seven-league boots and outstripped the prices of books, which come limping along behind. And seeing that we no longer bother with galoshes to protect even the most expensive footwear, it is understandable that book covers are no longer produced and hardly ever used any more. Protective covers and shields, often lovingly made, have not died out. However, they can only be found where there is something regarded as worth protecting: in the motor car, that home on four wheels.

- Rubber overshoes
- Protective covers for appliances
- Bonnet protector

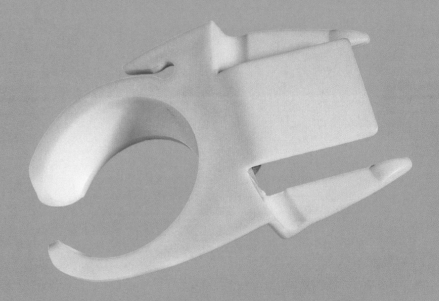

Plate clip

Make that cocktail party easier to handle

Who doesn't know what a hassle those sometimes crowded cocktail parties can be! You want to shake hands with your host to thank him for the invitation or give the person you're talking to a business card. But you've always got your hands full, what with your plate in one hand and your glass in the other.

Now our resourceful cocktail-party animal has solved the 'Where shall I put my glass' problem. The plate clip, weighing a mere 8 grams, can be attached to any plate and holds that delicious drink securely within reach.

[Auvisio, advertising copy]

Salvator

A cutlery rest for serving dishes

Our housewives will surely have found to their embarrassment that no matter how skilfully the serving is done at banquets, the cutlery slips from the rim of the dish into the gravy, which, besides making it necessary to replace the cutlery, is hardly designed to give one an appetite. Reason then to thank the resourceful minds who have succeeded in doing something about this nasty state of affairs and preventing the cutlery from wandering off so irresponsibly. The 'Salvator' cutlery rest does a thorough job. Made of a single piece of spring steel, it is easily attached to the dish, as shown in our pictures, and so simply and practically designed that any piece of cutlery will rest in it securely without slipping down, even if the dish is shaken vigorously, because it is held in place by the tapering projections.

   The simple nickel-plated or silver-plated models cost only 25 and 40 Pfennigs respectively, while the solid silver model costs 3 marks 50 pfennigs, making them affordable for every household. There is no doubt that this cutlery rest will soon be found wherever people value pleasant service.

[*Bibliothek der Unterhaltung und des Wissens* (Library of Entertainment and Knowledge), 1900]

Ivan Vladislavić

The habits of the Gorilla

Once bitten, twice shy When my car, a white Ford Meteor with eighty thousand kilometres on the clock, was stolen from outside my house, I immediately phoned my father. He listened sympathetically. Then he asked: 'Did you ever get yourself a Gorilla?'

He had been pestering me for months to buy a steering lock, and I had been putting it off. Now the car was gone. I was on the point of lying: Yes, Dad, I got myself a Gorilla, just as you suggested, but the thieves cut it off with an angle-grinder. Went through it like butter. But you cannot deceive my father about such things. 'No,' I said sheepishly. 'I meant to, I really did. But for one reason or another I never got round to it.'

'That's a pity.' There was a long, crackling silence. 'You know, the guys who make the Gorilla are so confident in their product, they offer the purchaser a special guarantee: if your car gets stolen with the Gorilla in place, they'll refund half the excess on your insurance. Ah well, perhaps you'll be more careful next time.'

The human bite With just six weeks left on the millennial clock, a Johannesburg computer specialist claimed that he had been savagely bitten in an attempted car hijacking. The 40-year-old man, who did not wish to be named in the newspaper report on the crime, was stopped at a traffic light in the early hours of the morning, with his car window slightly open. Two thieves reached into the vehicle and released the central locking mechanism. Then they both jumped into the car and began biting him. 'The one in front attacked his arm and bit it all the way up while the other started biting his neck and back, both of them drawing blood as they bit him.' The driver managed to get out of the car, but his assailants pursued him and continued to bite him. 'One was saying: "You taste good, white boy. I want to bite you more."' Eventually he managed to get back into his car and drive off. The man, who said that being bitten was worse than being attacked with a weapon, underwent medical tests and was given antibiotics and a tetanus injection. 'The doctor said a human bite is very poisonous.'[1]

The *Star* has a policy of not identifying individuals by race in their reporting. Here it makes no difference. Even if the phrase 'white boy' had been omitted, who would doubt that the computer specialist was white and the cannibals were black?

Birds of a feather The range of steering locks available in South Africa is impressive – the Wild Dog, the MoToQuip anti-theft lock, the Twistlok, the SL2 Auto-Lok, the Eagle Claw by Yale, the Challenger ... All these locks work on the same principle: they are attached to the steering wheel and immobilize the vehicle by preventing the wheel from being turned.

The locks also have the same basic design. There is a hardened steel shaft and an extendable bar. The two parts are connected by a locking ratchet mechanism and each part is furnished with a U-shaped hook or 'claw'. To engage the lock, you place the shaft diametrically across the steering wheel, with the bar retracted and the shaft claw around the rim. Then you extend the bar until the second claw fits around the opposite side of the rim. The ratchet engages automatically and locks the bar in place. If an attempt is made to turn the steering wheel now, the bar strikes the passenger seat, windscreen or door. To disengage the device, you insert the key in the lock and retract the bar, freeing the claws on both sides.

In some devices, the U-shaped hook on the shaft is replaced by a cork-screw hook, which is twisted around the rim of the steering wheel before the bar is engaged. The Twistlok, for instance, has such a hook, which is called the 'pigtail end'.

The selling points of the various locks are similar. They are made of tough, hardened steel which cannot be drilled, sawn or bent, and they are coated with vinyl to protect the interior fittings. They are easy to install, thanks to the automatic locking system, and highly visible to thieves; to heighten their visibility, and therefore their deterrent value, they are often brightly coloured. They have pick-resistant locks and high-security keys: the MoToQuip has 'cross point' keys; the Challenger has a 'superior circular key system'; and

Yale offers a 'pin tumbler locking system' with 10 000 different key combinations, and exerts strict control over the issuing of duplicates (by approved service centres only).

Some of these products draw explicitly on the symbolism of the predatory animal. The Eagle Claw, for instance, suggests a bird of prey: a raptor with the steering wheel in its clutches. The logo of the Wild Dog depicts a snarling Alsatian, more rabid and vicious than the conventional guard dog. The association with wild animals known for their speed, strength or ferocity is also found in other areas of the security industry: tigers, eagles and owls appear on the shields of armed-response companies, and rhinoceroses and elephants in the logos of companies that supply electrified fencing and razor wire.

The best of the breed The day after I acquired my new car, a bottle-green Mazda Midge, my father arrived on my doorstep. He was carrying a long package wrapped in mistletoe paper, although Christmas was a long way off. I knew at once what was in this package, but I pretended that I did not.

My father works in the motor trade and I have always respected his opinions about cars. He gave the Mazda a thorough check-up, doing all the things men do to determine the quality of a second-hand vehicle – kicking the tyres, bouncing up and down on the fenders to test the shock absorbers, looking in the cubbyhole, jiggling the steering wheel, gazing under the hood. He announced that I had made a sensible purchase. Then he gave me the present. It was a Gorilla.

He showed me how it worked, engaging and disengaging the device with practised ease. When it was my turn, the lock suddenly seemed like a test of perceptual intelligence, an educational toy of some kind. My fingers felt thick and clumsy: my hand-eye coordination had deserted me. The 'pigtail' kept slipping off the rim, like one of those magician's hoops that has a secret join in it. Finally I managed to engage the Gorilla.

'Don't worry, you'll get used to it,' he said. 'In the meantime, I have a couple of tips for you. Before you do anything else, you want to engage the standard steering lock that comes with the car. Just turn the wheel anticlockwise until it clicks in.

'Never install the device so that it's touching one of the windows. I know a guy who did that, and the bar expanded in the sun and cracked his windscreen.

'Then you must find a place to store the lock when it's not in use. I suggest you put it down here next to the seat. It's out of the way, and there's no danger of it getting caught under the pedals.

'Finally, you need to put a drop of oil in here from time to time. Just a drop, very occasionally. You don't want to get it on the upholstery.

'Right. Let's see you do it again.'

The nature of the beast The Gorilla has a personality of its own which sets it apart from the herd. It is made in one solid piece. There is no ratchet and no extension; instead the lock, like a jointed metal jaw, slides up and down on a single bar. This bar is made of naked stainless steel, cold to the touch and harsh on the eye. The 'pigtail' is bright red. The shiny metal bar is not coated with protective plastic, and so the device is leaner than the average lock, but if anything it looks stronger. It has nothing to hide. One is never tempted to wonder what material is concealed beneath the plastic skin. This is 'super hard steel', as the packaging puts it, designed to put an end to the 'monkey business of car theft'.

The brutal style of the device is echoed in one of the manufacturer's slogans: 'There's no substitute for brute force.' The pun on 'brute force' furthers a play of meanings already suggested by the trade name 'Gorilla'. Brute force is unthinking material force: there is no substitute for unbending steel. But it is also unfeeling animal force: there is no substitute for a powerful, dull-witted beast like a 'Gorilla'.

In English, mechanical devices are very commonly given the names of animals. In mechanics and mining, for instance, there are countless devices designated as 'dogs'. A 'dog' may be any form of spike, rod or bar with a ring, hook or claw for gripping, clutching or holding something. 'Dogs' form part of machines used in mines, sawmills and engineering works. 'Firedogs' are used to support wood in a fireplace, 'raft dogs' to hold together the logs forming a raft. Various machines and implements are also named 'monkeys', either arbitrarily or because of a supposed resemblance between the object and the animal. A 'monkey' is a crucible used in the manufacture of glass, for instance, or a weight used in the manufacture of iron. In the nautical environment, 'monkey' usually indicates that something has a peculiar use or location; it may also indicate that something is easy or simple. A 'monkey link', for instance, is an easily inserted repair link for a chain. This may be part of the derivation of 'monkey wrench', a tool which is a close cousin of the Gorilla.[2]

The ambiguous identity of a single device as dull object and dumb animal is captured in the logo of the Gorilla, which shows a stylized steering wheel gripped by two huge, humanoid paws, with the shaggy suggestion of an animal body in the background. Attaching this particular lock to the steering wheel is like leaving a Gorilla sitting in the driver's seat. Elsewhere on the packaging we read: 'Find it [your car] where you left it – get a "Gorilla" to protect it.' This slogan hints at a more covert layer of meaning. Colloquially a 'gorilla' is a powerfully built, brutish, aggressive man. So the device may be seen as a sort of simian watchman.

One day at the Jumbo The last day of 1998. I stop at the Jumbo Liquor Market in Op de Bergen Street on the way home to buy something for the

- Bruma
- Norwood
- Wits Mental Health Society, Benbow Street, Kensington
- Kitchener Avenue, Bezuidenhout Valley

New Year celebrations. Perhaps I should pick up a bottle of whisky? Or champagne?

The usual hawkers are gathered on the verandah outside. The tall cobbler and his pals. For years, he wore a springbok-skin cap, a hand-sewn thing that Crusoe would have given a sack of nails for, with flaps standing up like ears and a peak like a snout. With his bony cheeks and goatee, he looked like a buck himself or a part-time Pan. But then he abandoned the cap in favour of the conventional black imitation-leather Tyrolean.

While I'm engaging the Gorilla, a man appears at the window. I've never seen him before. He puts his face close to the two-inch gap between the top of the glass and the frame. A face made in the make-up department: a droll and drunken coloured face below a greasy cloth cap, missing teeth, smashed nose, boozy breath. 'I must watch this car, this place is full of skollies,' he tells me, gesturing vaguely towards the cobbler's circle and then pointing very definitely down Eleanor Street. 'Just last week they stole that car.' The car in question is a bakkie, drawing up that instant outside No. 12, having come the wrong direction up the one-way from Nourse Street. Two men get out of the bakkie and go into the house. What does he mean they stole that car last week? Who would have taken such a battered old pickup? And how did they get it back again so soon? Then logic turns his sentence inside out. He means it's a stolen vehicle. Those are the thieves! Probably a thief himself. Takes one to know one. I barge him aside with the door and go into the bottlestore.

Champagne bubbles up again briefly. But I think of the obligatory cork-popping in a year's time, and two years' time, and buy beer instead and a half-jack of J&B.

When I get back to my car, the coloured guy is hanging around on the other side of the street, shamefaced and jumpy, trying hopelessly to disguise his expectation. I dump the packet in the boot. I'm starting to regret my bad temper, starting to feel guilty. It's the season for giving, after all. I call him over and give him five bucks.

Now he wants to earn it, he wants to deserve my generosity. And he wants me to see the point too. 'I'm watching,' he says vehemently, 'I'm watching.' He points to his eyes, forefinger and little finger extended, the other two tucked into his fist by his thumb.

I get into the car.

'I'm watching.'

'Thank you,' I say through the diminishing gap, as I shut the door, 'thank you very much.'

His face is close to the glass again. Talking. Gesturing. Prongs of fore-finger and little finger waggling, roving, suggesting tireless vigilance. I stick the key in the Gorilla but it won't disengage: in my haste to get away, I've jammed the lock somehow. He goes on talking. I cannot ignore him. Elias

Canetti once said: 'I will be dead when I no longer hear what a person is telling me about himself.'[3] This cannot be what he had in mind. I open the window two inches. His face comes closer. He's tilting it to one side, so that I can see more of it through the gap. He wants me to know who he is, to look at him. He wants me to recognize him when I see him again. His nose is almost inside the car. As if he wants to squeeze in, to seize the hard edges of this opening, pull them wide, and climb through into the sweetly-scented interior. When they serviced the car last week, they spilled some green pellets in the ashtray that make it smell like new. New-car scent. I jiggle the Gorilla irritably and it finally pops loose. I put it in its place next to the seat. He's still talking, quickly, urgently, about thieves and cars and honesty and how we all have to work together against the scourge of skelms. Waving his arms around, pointing up and down Eleanor Street. Making peculiarly graceful movements with his hands, palms pressed together, as if he is praying or preparing to dive into a small pool.

I start the car but he won't let me go. He's talking and talking through the gap. Phrases out of the newspapers. Crime wave. Rainbow nation. Decent South Africans. Standing together. People of God. Thieves. Liars. Love. I start edging away from the kerb, cranking the steering wheel with my left hand and winding up the window with my right. My face is turned to him. We are staring at one another through the narrowing space.

'I'm not a security,' he says as the gap closes. 'I'm not a security, I swear, but I wanna work with the people of the land.'

The law of the jungle In 1998, 107 675 cars were stolen in South Africa (295 cars per day). There were 14 965 cars hijacked (41 per day).[4] The incidence of hijacking was directly related to the efficacy of vehicle security systems. The increasing application of alarms, electronic immobilizers, and steering and gear locks, especially to luxury motor cars, has made it almost impossible to steal an unoccupied, stationary car.

In 1998, a survey by the Labour Research Service in Cape Town found that the executive directors of South African companies earned an average of R 99 916 per month, or R 1.2 million a year, excluding bonuses and other benefits. A factory worker earning R 1 800 a month – the average minimum wage – would have taken five years to earn what the average company director earned in a month.[5] Yet these workers had to consider themselves fortunate, because 40 per cent of black South Africans were unemployed.

In 1999, crime cost South Africa an estimated R 30 billion (R 80 million a day). However, crime also created jobs. In the past two decades, the private security industry has grown faster than any other economic sector. At the end of August, according to Martin Schönteich of the Institute for Security

Studies, the official South African Police Service employed 127 000 people. By contrast, the private security industry employed between 300 000 and 350 000 people, and had an estimated annual turnover of R 11 billion.[6]

In August 1999, the prices of new cars available in South Africa ranged from R 38 086 for a Fiat Uno Mia to R 2 389 000 for a Ferrari 550 Maranello.[7] The prices of steering locks ranged from R 59 for the SL2 Auto-Lok to R 325 for the Gorilla. The price of brown bread was fixed by the government at R 1.90 a loaf.

The order of primates On the eve of the millennium, South Africa's new police commissioner, Jackie Selebi, entered the Brooklyn Police Station in Pretoria to make an inspection. According to subsequent news reports, the commissioner was not impressed with what he found. Incensed by the casual attitude of the charge-office staff and their failure to recognize him, he called Sergeant Jeanette Mothiba a 'fucking gorilla'. Sergeant Mothiba responded by laying a charge of crimen injuria against the commissioner.

The incident was widely reported. Some treated it as a joke or at worst a blunder. Others felt that the commissioner's language was not just inappropriate, but unforgivably derogatory and racist. It was an echo of the insulting 'baboon', used so often by white racists against black people, and all the more shocking in this instance because a prominent and powerful black man had used it against a black woman under his authority. One black female journalist wrote that the phrase conjured up the image of a gorilla mask, of the kind worn at fancy-dress parties, superimposed on a black woman's face. The image would linger, she said, and be used against other black women.[8]

After a fortnight of controversy, the Independent Complaints Directorate, to which the case had been referred, issued a report finding that Commissioner Selebi had not used the word 'gorilla' at all, but the word 'chimpanzee'. This word, unlike the word 'baboon', the report said, was not commonly used as an insult. Although it was safe to assume that the word had been used in an insulting fashion, it was not sufficient to warrant prosecution.

In its front-page report on the Directorate's findings, the *Star* ran an article titled 'What's the difference between a chimpanzee and a gorilla?'[9] The article pointed out that both are anthropoid apes of central West Africa, but whereas the chimp is 'gregarious and intelligent', the gorilla is 'stocky with a short muzzle and coarse dark hair'. The anthropoid apes belong to the order of primates, the article concluded, and so do human beings.

In the end, it was hard to say exactly who the joke was on. Commissioner Selebi, who had started this grotesque drama with his ill-judged comment. Or Sergeant Mothiba, who had vanished behind the headlines. Or the Independent Complaints Directorate, earnestly offering dictionary definitions as a legal defence. Or the reader, poking a stick through the bars at his own beastly nature.

▪ 'Gorilla'

Mastering the Gorilla I have employed the Gorilla for two years now. Engaging and disengaging it, once, twice, a dozen times a day. 'Never leave it off,' my father warned me. 'Even if you're just popping into the shop to buy a newspaper. It only takes a minute to steal a car.' The action has become second nature. I reach for the lock on the floor beside the seat, hook the pigtail over the rim, lower the arm, clamp the jaws. In a few seconds of smoothly choreographed movement, I extend my power over my property, laying claim to it in my absence, seizing it in leathery paws with an iron grip; and then I withdraw that power again and reduce it to its proper, meagre dimensions. I can do it in the dark. I could probably do it with one hand tied behind my back. I am a persuasive advertisement for the product and the security it offers.

[1] *Star*, 18 November 1999, p. 7.

[2] The universal spanner known as a 'monkey wrench' is called a 'Frenchman' in Germany, and an 'Englishman' in some other parts of the world.

[3] Elias Canetti, *The Torch in My Ear* (Farrar, Straus & Giroux, New York, 1982), p. 280.

[4] *Sunday Times*, 23 May 1999, p. 5.

[5] *Saturday Star*, 11 April 1998, p. 5.

[6] *Star*, 29 November 1999, p. 8.

[7] *Car Magazine*, August 1999, pp. 169, 172.

[8] *Sunday Times*, 16 January 2000, p. 14.

[9] *Star*, 18 January 2000, p. 1.

▪ Steering wheel lock

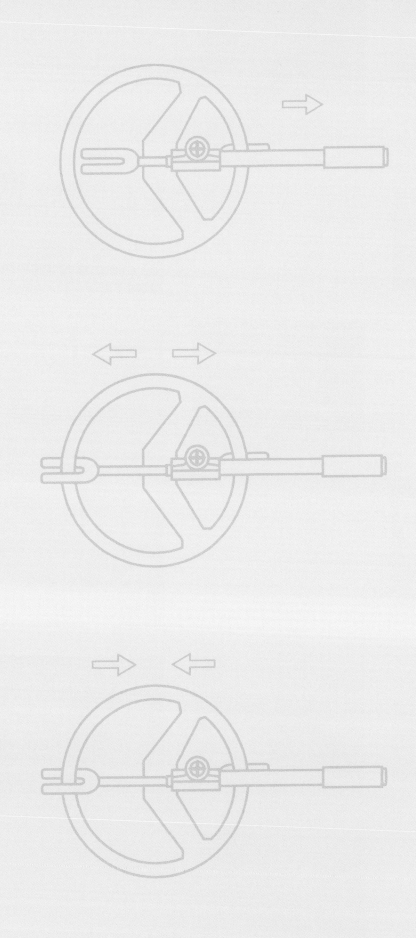

Hans-Joachim Ruckhäberle

On protectors and preservers

Objects in literature – not only fairy tales – can come to life. These 'things' then dance, even on Human Noses. Things move around, they speak one with another, they change names, they withdraw from human use, they refuse to fulfil their purposes just as they refuse their designations. These things free themselves from their names.

In real life things as objects stand in the way. They help and hinder. Vilém Flusser's concept of useful objects as hindrances 'which I use in order to advance', and which I thereby also consume, is an aspect of this. Things alter space and fix time. They are *dingfest* ('thingsure').

auf einem stuhl	on a chair
liegt ein hut.	lies a hat.
beide	both
wissen voneinander	know nothing
nichts	of each other
beide	both
sind	are
so dingfest.	so thingsure.

In Ernst Jandl's poem, hat and chair are things in themselves. But only in a poem are things simply there. In a poem, things ask for nothing, and nothing is asked of them. They are 'images'. The nature of their connection is the composition. The problems start when they need to become useful.

The hat is put on. The chair is occupied. They are no longer simply *'dingfest'*, they are made *'dingfest'* too.

Things owe their existence to their purpose. Without the question 'What for?' they would not exist. 'Their purpose precedes their existence and causes them to arise.' And yet they are not only purpose: 'Despite their total purposefulness – or even because of it – they are devoid of their own purposes.' (Hans Jonas)

And so a gulf opens up, a gulf that may be more or less wide and deep but is always present, between the purpose and the existence of things. This in-between makes the 'preservers' and 'protectors' necessary. There is an idea of purpose, of expected use, and there is the reality (materiality) of the object, which is more than its purpose. So there is a purpose, and there is something, which is distinct, the thing. And there is something, which is more, the value of the thing as a commodity.

Common to all 'protectors' and 'preservers' is that they do not change the purposes of things fundamentally; they are used when the purpose and the reality of the object do not coincide directly and unfailingly. And so we are concerned here only with protection and preservation, and not with improved use. Protection becomes necessary according to the extent of the gulf between the purpose and the thing: protection of things and protection against things. The necessity of the protection can be measured against the real risk. But it is different when it comes to the countless 'preservers', which appear rather when a thing fulfils its purpose particularly well, shall not be consumed in the process, and is supposed to stay 'beautiful'. The protective covering, the overshoe, the transparent cover and the screen saver do not make things better, they maintain them in a particular condition for longer. The objects are 'clothed' but not 'costumed'. Neither the 'protector' nor the 'preserver' fundamentally alters the idea of the things, but the nature of the things certainly changes: the limits of their usefulness become clear; time plays a role – the frequency and duration of use, and the moment of use itself.

Thus 'protectors' distinguish themselves from 'preservers', particularly as regards what precedes their application. The 'protector' protects against harm that would change not only the appearance but the form, while the 'preserver' seeks to keep something beautifully unchanged. Something may be preserved for sentimental reasons, out of respect, or because of its spiritual and material value. And so an ordinary, sensuous object becomes a rather curious creature. '... as soon as it emerges as a commodity' – Marx is talking about a table – 'it changes into a thing which transcends sensuousness ... and evolves out of its wooden brain grotesque ideas, far more strange, than if it were to begin dancing of its own free will.'

'Preservers' and 'protectors' make us aware that there is something 'artificial' about objects and how we deal with them. And they also make us conscious that we are not just designing 'new worlds' but also materializing these designs, that is, realizing them, and for this reason they stand opposed to other new designs, for instance, a three-year-old child's plan for passing directly through a space or a driver's wish to get into a car without dislocating anything.

Another possibility would be to understand ourselves as designs and to follow Alice into Wonderland, adapting to the way things are with the help of the 'Drink Me' bottle and the 'Eat Me' cake, in this case by getting bigger or smaller. This assumes, however, that like Alice we are willing to ask: 'Who in the world am I?'

■ 'Child Guard' safety plug

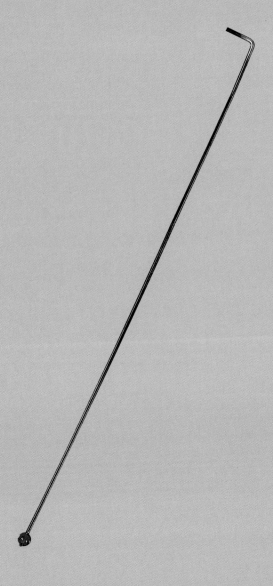

Tizio safety rod

Astina distanziatrice (cod. 305012)

'The fundamental design principle of this lamp is reduction. Tizio is an object you can take nothing away from and add nothing to without ruining the concept.'

[Ernesto Gismondi, President of Artemide]

In 1987/88, Tizio received an addition. The light no longer fulfilled the new safety regulations CEI 34/21 II. Richard Sapper designed a black rod with a small red plastic ball on the end: the safety rod. Since then Tizio has been sold all over the world with this addition. 'Not exactly the real thing visually,' says Sapper, and offers this advice:

'I personally always remove it from my lights. It was made so that you can just pull it off if you don't like it.'

[Richard Sapper]

Nose shield
for glasses

Izzy *(George Buck),*
in a deckchair on the beach in Coney Island
Oh here! Have a nose shield. Go on, take one. I found a
whole boxful under the boardwalk.

Harry Angel *(Mickey Rourke)*
There isn't much sun in the city right now.

Izzy
Yeah, but it keeps the rain off too.

(a bit later on the way back)

Harry Angel
Hey, thanks for the nose shield!

Izzy
That's ok.

Harry Angel
I'll need it where I'm going.

Izzy
Brooklyn?

Harry Angel
No. Louisiana.

[Dialogue from the film *Angel Heart*]

RING | CANDLE DRIPS

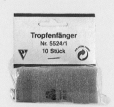

Tropfenfänger
Nr. 5524/1
10 Stück

Made in the U.S.A.

WAFFEN-VILLING

NITE IZE

MINI-FLASHLIGHT

GLOW-SPOT™

• LIGHT DIFFUSER
• SAFETY MARKER

HANG YOUR LIGHT!
Card & Split-Ring
Included

CAMPING:
Area Light
with Spot Beam

FISHING:
Preserves
Night Vision

EMERGENCY:
Warning, Attention
Signal

720384

Fits most AA size mini-flashlights

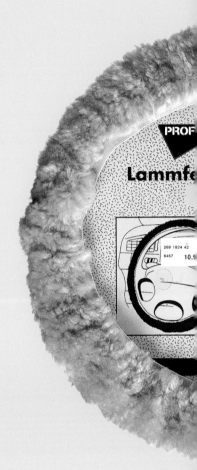

PROF

Lammfe

269 1624 42
6467   10,9

Art.-Nr. 75412

nkradbezug

uxe

● Echtes Lammfell
● passend für alle Lenkräder
● mit Gummizug für optimale Paßform
● rutschfest und angenehm griffig

4 008153 754128

auto-Zubehör

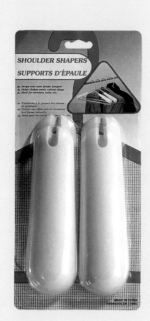

SHOULDER SHAPERS
SUPPORTS D'ÉPAULE

MADE IN CHINA

ALLES FÜR DIE
GASTRONOMIE

**Tischtuch-
bommeln**

Metro-Nr. 068441.5

4 008033 447553

Sporty-
Brillenclip

macht Ihre
Brille zur
Sportbrille

Sieve insert

Protection for urinals

Protects urinals against being blocked by cigarettes,
allows problem-free use of scented blocks. As the
shapes of urinals vary enormously, the sieve can be
adapted easily if necessary by bending or cutting it
to size.

[Dr Becher, packaging copy]

Endless Aid

or the third aid, the fourth aid ...

1 In the autumn of 1970, I went to university in Berlin and very eagerly began my German Studies course. Lost as I often was in the fog of my sketchy German, I bought myself a little crimson Suhrkamp volume with the title *Materialien zu Bertolt Brechts 'Der Gute Mensch von Sezuan'*. It was only when I found out that there was a play by Brecht with the title *The Good Woman of Szechwan* that I realized how pointless this purchase was. As I had neither read nor seen the play, the commentaries in the book of secondary material did not help me in the slightest. This experience, which took place many years ago now, came back to me again when I was discussing with Jörg Adam and Dominik Harborth the things they call *Helfershelfer*: dependent, quasi-'underage' objects that cannot exist independently and are subordinate to other objects, which they are supposed to complete, improve or perfect. They do not stand out at first, these 'second aids', whether in bookshops or in supermarkets. In the second aid, a useful object which belongs to the order of commodities, we recognize something that Guy Debord said about commodities in general, 'our old enemy, ... who knows so well how to seem at first glance something trivial and obvious, while on the contrary it is so complex and so full of metaphysical subtleties'.[1]

2 It is surprising to what extent the authors of the various articles and interviews in this book agree that second aids are to be seen as an independent category within the world of objects. Significantly, in their letters to the authors and in their interviews, when it came to describing the product group that interested them, Jörg Adam and Dominik Harborth used an existing word: *Helfershelfer*.[2] It is a metaphor clear to everyone in this context: by bending the meaning of the word a little, on the one hand, they give a new dimension to *'Helfershelfer'* – a helpful object, applied to another helpful object;[3] and on the other, they play with the composition of the word itself. Incidentally, when the products referred to here appear in catalogues, they are usually also denoted by compounds: 'car visor organizer' *(Sonnenblenden-Butler)*; 'underarm sweat guard' *(Achselschweißstopp)*; 'Door-mounted coat rack' *(Türhakenleiste)*; or 'brassiere fastening inset' *(Büstenhalter-Verschlusseinsatz)*. Each of these concepts has been formed in the same way: there is a chain of terms built around a central core. In this instance, the inventiveness of German tinkerers and designers accords perfectly with the German language: on the one hand, technical elements are combined endlessly to improve or modify the function of an object; and on the other, terms are strung together with the same gain in precision: *Helfershelfershelfer* (second aid, third aid) ... etc.

3 Actually, Adam and Harborth do not define the second aid in exactly the same way. Whereas Adam talks of an object that has no function in itself, Harborth sees the 'second aid' as an object that has to adapt itself to another. If one considers its functionality alone, that is, its use value, it appears to be practically impossible to distinguish the second aids precisely from other objects. Is a kitchen appliance with its accessories a distinct object presented together with its second aids, or are we talking about a single product conceived as a whole? Or a tie, which is useless without a shirt, and the shape of which has been so precisely adapted to the collar that it can disappear underneath it – is this a second aid? What about a computer program, or a remote control for the television, or the *Materialien zu Bertolt Brechts 'Der Gute Mensch von Sezuan'*?

Jean Baudrillard ends his text *The System of Objects* with a definition of consumption as 'the virtual totality of all objects and messages presently constituted in a more or less coherent discourse'.[4] Further on, he says: 'In order to become object of consumption, the object must become sign.' If one applies this definition to the second aid, one can see in it an 'object-sign' like other 'object-signs', which 'draws its coherence, and therefore its reason for being, from an abstract and systematic relationship to all other object-signs. Subsequently it is "personalized", becomes a series etc. ... Finally it is consumed – not in its materiality but in its difference.'[5] The second aids, beautifully packaged and prominently displayed in the supermarkets, pretend to be 'saviours' of objects and faithful helpers. But appearances are deceptive: the second aid is an object-sign that may be just as treacherous and seductive and disappointing as any other commodity.

Apart from its abstract relationship to all other object-signs, the second aid enters into a relationship with a specific object-sign, without which it could not exist, and the defects and inadequacies of which it exposes. The drip-catcher reveals the imperfection of the teapot that stains the tablecloth, the spoiler the instability of the sports car when it exceeds a certain speed. It is hardly surprising that designers are not very fond of second aids, which constantly remind them that the object-signs are faulty, that the perfection of their shape is relative, and that they may disappoint the consumer, blinded by the passion to consume, at any time.

4 The second aid carries the evidence of its connection to another object in itself; its function and occasionally also its shape derive directly from the object it is designed to complement. So the 'shower rose' takes the shape of the shower head, the 'headlight covers' the shape of the headlights. As consumer goods, second aids awaken the need for another, absent object. They thus refer to an absence, and in this they resemble Marcel Duchamp's ready-mades, which are all concerned with the absence of other objects: the absence of tyre and tube in the *Bicycle Wheel (Roue de bicyclette)* or the absence of bottles in the *Bottle Rack (Sèche-Bouteilles)*.[6] Just as Duchamp gave his ready-made snow shovel *(pelle à neige)* the subtitle *In Advance of the Broken Arm (En Prévision du bras cassé)*, so we buy a 'gutter guard' in advance of the damage to the gutters which might be caused by the next storm. Which is not to say that we consume commodities in the same way we perceive art works (although, in today's art market, one might ask, why not?); no, the logic Marcel Duchamp pursues in his ready-mades – provoking attention through the perception of an absence – is rather exploited in the consumer world, where absence is consciously orchestrated to awaken the desires of the consumer. To this extent, the second aid is a pure consumer object, freed of any use value, which, in itself, it lacks entirely. Second aids awaken the need for other objects, whose absence they themselves reveal, and they are therefore real *machines célibataires* within the consumer world.

▪ Second aids in the supermarket

5 Can a second aid fill the emptiness which yawns between the finished object and the insatiable desires of the consumer? One could add an endless number of aids to the second aids, and still a gap would remain to be filled. Not least because our wishes change with time and our changing needs, and the space they open up is constantly moving. An object is not adapted to the needs of the consumer, by setting another object aside for him. It rather has to adapt itself flexibly to the needs of the consumer. In the eighteenth century, the engineer Jacques de Vaucanson invented the first fully automatic loom. Although it was perfectly conceived and worked properly, it did not achieve the success that was hoped for. Instead, the mechanic Joseph Marie Jacquard of Lyon went down in history, having suggested a definite improvement to the working of this machine: a device with perforated cardboard plates, relatively simple to operate, which Vaucanson had not provided for his loom and which made it possible to programme weaving patterns. Today Vaucanson's invention, his loom, bears the name of the person who invented the second aid, which merely improved the way it worked. This kind of second aid corresponds to what we now call the 'interface' – all those aids which facilitate communication between the object and its user.

The concept of the *Helfershelfer*, as Jörg Adam and Dominik Harborth mean it to be understood, refers to objects, and thus deviates from the original sense of the word, which denotes the comrade of an assistant, or an accomplice.

It is very likely that the second aids of the future will not be objects that make up for defects, but rather strategies that manage the problems of communication and interfacing. With their publication and exhibition devoted to second aids, Adam and Harborth have undoubtedly defined a new semantic field within the world of objects. One of the main concerns – and merits! – of their project was to encourage a new and closer relationship between producers, products, users and designers. To this extent, they too, as practitioners and theorists, are 'second aids', perhaps even the second aids of tomorrow's design.

[1] Guy Debord, *Die Gesellschaft des Spektakels* [The Society of the Spectacle] (Edition Tiamat, Berlin, 1996), p. 31.

[2] The following discussion revolves around the original German term translated elsewhere in this text as 'second aid', namely *'Helfershelfer'*, literally, a 'helper's helper', an assistant or accomplice.

[3] Thus my suggestion that 'second aids' be termed *'Compléments d'objet'* in French. *'Complément d'objet'* (in French: accusative object) is just as ambiguous as *'Helfershelfer'*.

[4] Jean Baudrillard, 'The System of Objects', in M. Poster (ed.), *Selected Writings* (Stanford University Press, Stanford, 1988), p. 22.

[5] ibid., p. 22.

[6] See Gérard Wajcman, *L'Objet du siècle* (Paris, 1998), pp. 81ff.

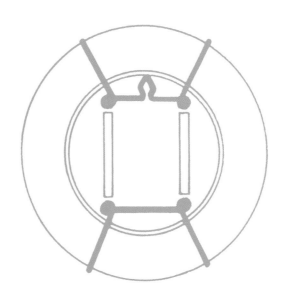

Contributors

Willi Aichert Born 1955, studied Industrial Design at Darmstadt University of Applied Sciences. First employed at Rubbermaid GmbH in Dreieich. Designer at Fackelmann since 1983.

Arzu Alagöz Born 1969, studied at the University of Marburg. 1997–2000: employed as a qualified saleswoman in product management of household goods at Fackelmann.

Jürgen W. Braun Born 1938, studied Law at the Universities of Bonn and Paris; first and second state exams in Düsseldorf; five years in Business Management, Export: Daimler-Benz, Stuttgart; five years in Sales Management, Bearings: NTN, Düsseldorf; Managing Director of the fittings manufacturer FSB (Franz Schneider Brakel) since July 1981.

François Burkhardt Born 1936 in Winterthur, studied Architecture at the Swiss Federal Institute of Technology, Lausanne and at the School of Fine Art, Hamburg. 1971–84: Head of the International Design Centre, Berlin. 1973–80: Board of the Bauhaus Archive, Berlin. 1974–80: Board of the German Design Council, Darmstadt. 1984–90: Director of the Centre des Création Industriel at the Pompidou Centre, Paris. 1990–91: Juror for Architecture at the Academy Schloss Solitude, Stuttgart. Professor in the School of Fine Art, Saar, since 1992; Director of the architecture and design magazine *Domus* since 1996. Conception of numerous exhibitions in the areas of fine arts, architecture and design. Adviser to institutions and companies in Germany, France, Belgium, Italy and Austria.

Christian Donle Born 1964, studied Law (doctorate). Scholarship at the Max Planck Institute in Munich to study foreign and international law on patents, copyright and competition. Lawyer, partner in the law firm Seelig & Preu, Bohlig, in Berlin, since 1990.

Hajo Eickhoff Born 1946, studied Philosophy, History of Art, and History (doctorate). Various teaching posts, among others at the Berlin University of the Arts. Consults in the furniture industry (on chairs and other seating). Author of *Himmelsthron und Schaukelstuhl: Die Geschichte des Sitzens*. Texts on the theory and history of culture, on the inner design of the human being, and on literature. Works as a freelance author and curator in Berlin.

Udo Engelke Born 1961, trained in sales at Thomashilfen since 1983. Initially in the field as Technical Adviser to institutions, now Sales and Marketing Manager.

Hans Jürgen Forster Born 1965, three-year training as office salesman at Versandhaus Walz, the mail-order firm, then deployed in Purchasing. Head of Purchasing Department since 1992, and Area Manager for purchasing in the Far East since 1998.

Bernd Gallandi Born 1959, trained as a photographer at the Lette School, Berlin, 1978–80. Founded Gallandi Photo Design Studio in Berlin, 1984. Works in advertising and architecture.

Hans Höger Born 1960, doctorate in History of Art on 'Continuity and Method in the Work of Ettore Sottsass Jr'. 1992–97: Technical Head and Secretary of the German Design Council, Frankfurt. 1994: appointed by Foreign Office as Exhibition Commissioner for the German pavilion at the 19th Milan Triennale. 1996: Curator of the congress programme 'Attitudes for the New Millennium' at the 43rd International Design Conference in Aspen, Colorado. Since 1998, publicist and adviser in Milan; teaches Design and Visual Arts in the 'Economy, Culture and Communication' course at Bocconi University, Milan.

Günter Höhne Born 1943, worked for many years as an editor in radio and print, before becoming a freelance journalist in Berlin. Has focused for the past 25 years on historical and current developments in design and architecture. 1984–89: Chief Editor of the East Berlin design magazine *form+zweck*. Since 1995, Co-editor of the Frankfurt magazine on design and theory *form diskurs*. Author of numerous articles in books. Member of design juries. Teaching posts in Berlin and Hanover.

Jean-Baptiste Joly Born 1951 in Paris, pursued German Studies in Paris and at the Free University Berlin. Honorary Professor at the Academy of Arts, Berlin-Weissensee. Since 1989, Director of the Academy Schloss Solitude, Stuttgart.

Wolfgang Pauser Born 1959 in Vienna, studied Philosophy, History of Art, Law (LLD). Works as a freelance essayist with a focus on day-to-day culture. Columnist for *Die Zeit* since 1994. 1998 Essay Prize for the State of Lower Saxony. Teaches Theory of Architecture at the Vienna University of Technology; undertakes product analyses for companies from a cultural-studies perspective. *Dr. Pausers Autozubehör* was published by Sanssouci (Zürich) in 1999. Lives in Vienna.

Hans-Joachim Ruckhäberle Born 1947, dramaturge and director. Since 1993, Professor of Directing and Dramaturgy at the Academy of Arts, Berlin-Weissensee, in the field of Stage Design. 1986: Max Kade Professor at Princeton University. 1983–93: Chief Dramaturge and member of the artistic management at the Münchner Kammerspiele. Since 1989, member of the Academy of Arts, Berlin. 1997–99: Chairman of the Jury, Academy Schloss Solitude, Stuttgart. Since 2001, Chief Dramaturge at the Bayerisches Staatsschauspiel, Munich.

Bruno Sacco Born in Udine, studied Mechanical Engineering at the Polytechnic of Turin. With Daimler-Benz since 1958. In 1974 appointed Chief Engineer. Head of Design from 1975 until his retirement in April 1999. Major awards: 1995 Premio Mexico, Mexico DF; 1996 Designer's Designer, Car, Warwick Castle; 1997 Honored Designer (Lifetime Design Achievement Award), Detroit; 1997 Lucky Strike Designer Award, Berlin.

Karin Scheffold Born 1967, three-year training as office saleswoman at Versandhaus Walz, the mail-order firm. 1987–89: worked there in wholesale and foreign trade. 1989–92: trained as a photographer, and worked in salaried employment and freelance as a photographer, picture and text editor. 1998–99: seasonal work as a shepherdess in the Swiss Alps. Since 1994, advertising assistant at Versandhaus Walz, 'Die moderne Hausfrau' department.

Helmut Staubach Born 1949, studied Design in Schwäbisch Gmünd and Kassel. Member of the scientific staff at the Institute for Industrial Design, University of Hanover. 1984–89: teaching posts at the University of Hanover, the Darmstadt University of Applied Sciences, and the Berlin University of the Arts. 1989–93: Professor at the Darmstadt University of Applied Sciences. Since 1993, Professor for Design at the Academy of Arts, Berlin-Weissensee, School of Art and Design. 1980–88: freelance work in Hanover; office in Berlin since 1988. 1998–99: Juror for Design at the Academy Schloss Solitude, Stuttgart.

Ivan Vladislavić Born 1957 in Pretoria, writer and editor. Studied Literature at the University of the Witwatersrand. First short stories in early eighties. Work has been translated into German, French and Serbo-Croat. 1999: scholarship at the Academy Schloss Solitude, Stuttgart. Books include

Missing Persons, *Propaganda by Monuments*, *The Folly* and *The Restless Supermarket*, which won the Sunday Times Fiction Prize in 2002. Co-edited *blank_Architecture, apartheid and after*. Lives and works in Johannesburg.

Margit Weinberg Staber Writes on art, and works as a publicist in design and architecture. Studied at the Ulm College of Design. Guest curator at the Haus für konstruktive und konkrete Kunst, Zürich, and member of the Board of Trustees. 1990–91: Juror for Design at the Academy Schloss Solitude, Stuttgart, and member of the Advisory Board until 1998. Lives in Zürich.

Thomas Werle Born 1969, studied Law, member of staff of the publishing house Gruner + Jahr in Hamburg. Since 1999, lawyer in the firm of Seelig & Preu, Bohlig, in Berlin.

Bernhard Wördehoff Born 1929, journalist. 1976–86: Chief Editor at Radio Germany, Cologne. Has since produced numerous pieces for print and broadcast. Author of several books, most recently *Flaggenwechsel* (1990), *Das gab's doch mal* (1994), *Picknick mit Eckermann* (1999) and *Sage mir, Muse, vom Schmause …* (2000).

Herbert Woyna Born 1941, state-certified mechanical engineering technician. Employed as a Design Engineer in the Development Department for remote-controlled aircraft at the Bölkow company; then worked for 20 years in technical field service. Since 1990/91, initially as a hobby and sideline, then as his main occupation, has published the magazine *Der Ideenmarkt*. In 1995, in line with trends and changes in content, this magazine for inventors and marketers was renamed *Patent- und Ideenmarkt*.

Judith Zaugg Born 1970 in Bern, studied Graphic Design at the School of Design, Bern. Since 1991, illustration and design of CDs, books, posters, logos, websites etc. Exhibitions in Stuttgart, Hamburg, Frankfurt, Erlangen, Helsinki, Bern, Lucerne, Schaffhausen, Langenthal, Basel, Zürich and New York. 1997: scholarship at the Academy Schloss Solitude, Stuttgart. Picture book *Bruno Orso fliegt ins Weltall* (MaroVerlag, Augsburg). 2000: 'Lernen mit dem Computer', illustrations for *ZEIT Punkte*. Lives and works in Bern.

Thanks

We are very grateful to:

Jean-Baptiste Joly for his support and many stimulating discussions.

Helmut Staubach for guiding our project from Berlin and for visiting us in Stuttgart.

Werner Irro for his expert advice and support.

Doris Adam, Ilse Babel, Angelika Baur, Matthias Berke, Rudolf-Dieter Friedrich, Monika Reutter, Jeannette Stoschek, Ada Maria, Solveig and Leopold for their acting skills in the illustrative photos.

Minky Schlesinger for the photos in 'The habits of the Gorilla'.

Christine Braunschweig for the transcription of the interviews and her support.

Thierry Blondeau, Georg Holzer, Jean-Baptiste Joly, Anna Martin and Jeannette Stoschek for translating the correspondence.

Artemide Germany for visual material and research.

We would also like to thank:

Wolfgang Adam
Martina Gallandi
Françoise Joly
Annette Kulenkampff
Ernst Ludwig
and the staff of the Academy Schloss Solitude

Lenders

We thank the following companies and individuals for their generous support:

Fackelmann GmbH+Co., Hersbruck
FTA, Film- und Theaterausstattung GmbH, Hamburg
HM Tuning GmbH, Pfedelbach
IMS Melchert, Bockhorn
Magazin GmbH, Stuttgart
Manufactum, Hoof + Partner KG, Waltrop
Meyra GmbH+Co.KG, Vlotho
MVG Vertrieb, Ingolstadt
Technotrade GmbH+Co., Philippsthal
Thomashilfen, Bremervörde
Vela Werbeartikel GmbH+Co. KG, Bad Salzuflen
Versandhaus Walz GmbH, Bad Waldsee
WMF Württembergische Metallwarenfabrik AG, Geislingen/Steige

Doris Adam, Düsseldorf
Paul Aubele, Obergröningen
Familie Friedrich, Solitude
Achim John, Dettingen
Rudolf Kraus, Karlsruhe
Karl Bernd Vilter, Staden

References

Translations:
'Things are whole parts' by Wolfgang Pauser was translated by Steve Gander.
'Endless Aid' by Jean-Baptiste Joly was originally translated from French into German by Helga Kopp.

Quotations:
p. 6, Socrates and Protagoras in dialogue, from *The Dialogues of Plato*, translated by Benjamin Jowett (London, 1952).

p. 8, Excerpt from Sigmund Freud, *Civilization and Its Discontents*, translated by James Strachey (New York, 1961).

p. 39, Excerpt from the Medical Review Board catalogue of assistive devices, Essen.

p. 47, Excerpts from the websites of various manufacturers and dealers.

p. 48, Chin rest, in Paul Otto Apian-Bennewitz, *Die Geige, der Geigenbau und die Bogenverfertigung* (Weimar, 1892).

p. 103, Salvator, in *Bibliothek der Unterhaltung und des Wissens*, vol. 5 (Stuttgart, 1900).

p. 118, Gismondi, in Uta Brandes, *Richard Sapper – Werkzeuge für das Leben* (Göttingen, 1993).

p. 118, Sapper, in Hans Höger, *Die Tizio-Leuchte von Richard Sapper* (Frankfurt, 1997).

p. 123, *Angel Heart*, Winkast-Union Production, Carolco International, NY, 1987.

All the texts were written specially for this book, except for:
Margit Weinberg Staber, 'Design: ... it's dripping', which first appeared in German in the magazine *Ideales Heim/Atrium* (Schaffhausen, 1994).

Bernhard Wördehoff, 'The pencil extender' and 'The book cover' both first appeared in German in *Das gab's doch mal* (Vienna, 1994).

Sources of images

All the photos are by Bernd Gallandi, except for:

Artemide GmbH, Hilden, p. 119.

Versandhaus Walz GmbH, Bad Waldsee, pp. 54, 74, 101 (centre).

Fackelmann GmbH+Co, Hersbruck, pp. 34/35.

Minky Schlesinger, Johannesburg, pp. 107–110.

Porzellanfabrik Weiden Gebr. Bauscher, Weiden, p. 17.

A.W. Faber-Castell GmbH, Stein/Nuremberg, p. 44.

Fritz Terofal, *Meeresfische in europäischen Gewässern*, Steinbachs Naturführer (Munich, 1986), pp. 32/33.

Winkast-Union Production, Carolco International, NY, 1987, p. 123.

All photos illustrating use are by Andrea Vilter.

... You need it every day

Beautifies every teapot and coffee pot

Our drip-catcher made of moltopren sponge protects your tablecloth against troublesome stains!

   Suitable for all teapots and coffee pots. Simply fasten the rubber band to the handle of the pot and stretch it over the lid, until you can put the sponge around the spout. This will hold the lid in place during pouring too. After use, just clean the sponge easily and simply with the washing-up.

[Wenco, packaging copy]